CONTENTS

BROADCAST WRITING WORKBOOK

Daniel E. Garvey
California State University
Long Beach

William L. Rivers
Stanford University

BROADCAST WRITING WORKBOOK

Longman Inc., 1560 Broadway, New York, N.Y. 10036
Associated companies, branches, and representatives
throughout the world.

Developmental editor: Gordon T.R. Anderson
Editorial and Design Supervisor: Frances Althaus
Manufacturing and Production Supervisor: Anne Musso

Manufactured in the United States of America

9 8 7 6 5 4 3

PREFACE

This workbook is designed to help you learn broadcast writing by doing just that--writing. The textbook <u>Broadcast Writing</u> can be used with the workbook, but there is sufficient basic information in this workbook for it to be used by itself.

In the course of a single semester you will probably not do all the exercises in this workbook. (You should be able to do two or three from each chapter.) Don't forget about the other exercises after the course is completed. If you find you have a problem with some particular form of broadcast writing, go back to the appropriate chapter and do some additional exercises. Or if you find you want more experience in a particular kind of broadcast writing, try a few more exercises in that section. And you can always do some of the remaining exercises as a refresher course from time to time.

The important thing is to keep writing. The more you write, the better you will get, especially if you pay attention to criticisms of your work by more experienced writers.

The first two chapters of this workbook are particularly important because they give you the rules that govern broadcast writing. Study these chapters carefully, and give particular attention to the exercises.

Give each form of writing in the book a fair chance. Not everyone wants to write a commercial or a news program. But everything you learn about writing will make you a better writer. So give each exercise your best. You'll be glad you did.

When people speak of writing, they are usually thinking of writing
for the print media--books, magazines, or newspapers. Maybe you've
already taken a course in writing for one of these media. If you
have, you'll find that many of the techniques you learned will work
just as well for broadcast writing. Writers in all media are trying
to achieve many of the same goals.

Nevertheless, don't feel you are at a disadvantage if you have
not taken other writing courses. Some things learned in other
writing courses must be *un*learned in order to write good broadcast
copy.

THE WORLD OF BROADCASTING
Students often think of broadcast writing in terms of the dramas and
comedies they see on network television. That is really a very small
part of the total world of broadcast writing. Broadcast writers
prepare news, advertising, public relations material, and public
service announcements. They write complete scripts and semiscripted
material. Some work in writers' hideaways, alone with their type-
writers and their thoughts; others work as producers, disc jockeys,
or program hosts.

The important thing for you to remember is that almost every
word you hear on radio, television, or cable was written--or at least

1

planned by a writer. Writing for prime-time television programs is a relatively small field; writing for broadcasting is not.

This book provides an opportunity to work with the major kinds of broadcast writing. It gives you a chance to learn which kinds you can do best and which appeal to you the most. Don't rule out any broadcast writing until you have given yourself a fair trial at writing each form of it. You cannot expect to do a professional job on your first attempt. Nor should you expect to become a professional broadcast writer after taking a single course in broadcast writing.

What you will learn in this book is the scope of broadcast writing and the basics of the major forms of broadcast writing. Your own talent and your willingness to work will ultimately determine your success in broadcast writing. But you can gain a head start by learning basic skills in this course and by discovering those areas of broadcast writing for which you are best suited.

We'll begin this workbook with the assumption that everyone is starting from scratch, that all you really know about broadcast writing is what you've seen on the television screen or heard on the radio.

Where do you start? You begin by examining the basic unit of all writing--the sentence. How does the sentence used in broadcasting differ from the sentences you have learned to write in other forms?

THE BASIC STRUCTURE OF BROADCAST SENTENCES

Ernest Hemingway, whose writing won him a Nobel Prize for literature, once advised writers: "The first and most important thing of all, at least for writers today, is to strip language clean, to lay it bare down to the bones." That advice makes as much sense today as it did when Hemingway wrote it. It can be reduced to three simple words: Use language simply. It is good advice for any writer, and especially good advice for a broadcast writer.

Choosing Words And Phrases

Think about the words you write. Your professors may rattle off words like "disaggregate" and "pretentiousness." It is normal for you, as a writer, to admire a large vocabulary, but never use a broadcast script to show off your vocabulary. Use words that your audience is sure to understand.

Think of the phrases you choose. Does your script call for a character to say, "The king has issued an edict to the effect that"? Why use "to the effect that"? Time is the shortest commodity in broadcasting. Can you afford to waste the extra seconds it takes to say "to the effect" when "the king has issued an edict that" says the same thing? Should a character be concerned with "the subject of charity" when just "charity" will do? It may seem a minor point, but the wasted seconds mount up. Good broadcast writers make sure every word in a script is there for a reason.

Simple English

When you're attempting to convert a cliche into an original phrase and don't have time to fashion one, use plain, unself-conscious English. For example, during World War II, the director of CBS News posted this memo in the CBS newsroom:

> This morning within the space of 30 seconds I heard German submarines called submarines, U-boats, submersibles, and underseas craft. The word submarines was used only once. It should have been used more often. But, my God, submersibles! That word should never be used. . .

Even though that was written about forty years ago, it should still be posted in the newsroom. The director knew that his employees were writing to be heard by many people. Even listeners who knew the word submersibles would have to think about the word for a few seconds; meanwhile, the newscaster would have continued his sentence.

For all broadcast writing, simplicity is essential. Examine
the clean, direct dialog of dramas by Rod Serling. Listen to the
uncomplicated writing in most situation comedies. Examine recorded
examples of masters of radio drama like Norman Corwin, great writers
of radio comedy like Don Quinn, or the unadorned journalism of Edward
R. Murrow. Simplicity and eloquence are not enemies, they are allies.
Mark Twain wrote: "As to the adjective, when in doubt, strike it out."
In commercials, where adjectives are often a key element, they are
chosen with the greatest care and never compete with unneeded
adjectives. Make every word in your script serve a purpose.

WRITING SENTENCES

When you sit down at the typewriter to write a broadcast script, it
is easy to slip into the mistake of simply thinking of yourself as a
writer instead of a broadcast writer. In your memory may lurk
beautiful examples of print writing. Take, for example, this passage
from the book, Coming into the Country, by New Yorker writer John
McPhee:

> Drifting now--a canoe, two kayaks--and thanking God it is not
> my turn in either of the kayaks, I lift my fishrod from the
> tines of a caribou rack (lashed there in mid-canoe to the
> duffel) and send a line flying toward a wall of bedrock by
> the edge of the stream.

Beautiful. You can see, feel, and smell the scene. Exactly the way
you want your broadcast audience to react to your writing. But would
it work? Not for television dialog. You could use some of it to
describe the scene and some to describe action for your actors, but
it's not a line for someone to recite while sloshing about in a
canoe. Ah, you say, but it would work for radio. Don't count on it.

1. John McPhee, Coming into the Country (Farrar, Straus & Giroux: New
   York, 1976), p. 5.

It makes too many demands on a listener. It's full of words that may be unfamiliar--"kayaks," "caribou rack," "duffel"--and it tries to cram too many ideas into one sentence. For example, the parenthetical phrase "lashed there in mid-canoe to the duffel" breaks the listener's train of thought. When the action of the sentence continues "and send a line flying," the listener may have to stop and think, "What line?" There are too many details to keep in mind. As beautifully crafted as the sentence is, it is a poor model for broadcast writing. It is meant to be read, not heard.

Not even all the material you see or hear broadcast provides good examples for your writing. Take, for example, CBS sportscaster Haywood Hale Broun. No one would deny he is a successful broadcast writer in his field, but should you take him as a model? No. At least, not while you are learning your craft. Take this sentence Broun wrote on the eve of the World Series: "Not since the dancing madness of the fourteenth century has there been such unrestrained mirth and mania as can be invoked by the New York Mets." The sentence makes too many demands on the audience. How much do you know about the "dancing madness of the fourteenth century"? Broun can get away with it because the audience has become accustomed to his style. Broun sums it up succinctly: "People have told me they saw a show of mine and didn't know what all the words meant, but they enjoyed it."

A young writer, starting out, has little hope of finding such a tolerant audience. Nor did Broun's style catch on quickly. It took time to build an audience that appreciated Broun for his personality and his sometimes-hard-to-grasp wit. Broun is an individual, and perhaps one of the few who can write as he does and still lure viewers. If you're attracted to Broun's style, don't try to learn broadcast writing by imitating him. Eventually you may become another Broun and a great broadcast writer, but first you must write simply.

The typical broadcast sentence follows the standard English pattern: subject, verb, direct object. It has been likened to the "See Spot run" sentences of children's readers. Of course, too much of anything, including simple sentences, gets to be a bore. But you must always keep in mind that your listener has only one chance to get what you are saying. The listener cannot reread your sentence if he doesn't understand it the first time.

Don't be misled by the axiom that broadcast writing is "conversational." It should sound conversational, but real conversation is often wordy and ambiguous. There is no time in broadcasting to use more words than needed, and there is no place in broadcast writing for unintentional ambiguity. Listen carefully to the dialog in any good broadcast drama. Almost every word is there for a purpose. The trick is to write concisely and still have it sound like everyday conversation.

Naturally, broadcast news writing must have the same conciseness. It is not presented as dialog, but it still should sound conversational. A broadcast news story should not read like this brief story from the Los Angeles Times:

> Fifty-seven people died in California traffic accidents during the four-day New Year's holiday weekend, 31 fewer than the record number killed during the four-day Christmas holiday weekend, the California Highway Patrol reported. The 88 deaths during the Christmas holidays were the most ever in California on a holiday weekend.

Try reading that aloud to a friend. You'll discover two things. First, the copy is hard to read aloud, and second, your friend won't be able to keep track of what you are saying. The sentences are not simple, and the style is not conversational. A broadcast newsperson

2. "The State," Los Angeles Times, January 3, 1980, sec. 1, p. 3.

might write the story like this:

> It was another tragic yearend on California's highways. Traffic accidents claimed 57 lives over the 4-day weekend. If there's any element of <u>good</u> news in those figures, it's that the death toll was way down from last week's record. Over the 4-day Christmas weekend, 88 people died on California's highways-- more than any other weekend in state history.

In the broadcast version, the writer approached the story this way: The first sentence must introduce the subject. The details can come later, and the shorter the sentences, the easier it will be for the listener to follow.

A few grammatical rules were violated to maintain a conversational sound. For example, the last sentence, grammatically, should read "more than <u>on</u> any other weekend." But the key element of the writing is simplicity.

Choosing Verbs

Your writing will sound much more forceful if you use active verbs instead of passive verbs. Because students get so little training in formal grammar these days, that statement may need some explaining. An <u>active</u> <u>verb</u>, or a verb in the <u>active</u> <u>voice</u>, is a verb that tells what the subject of the sentence is doing. A <u>passive</u> verb, or one in the <u>passive</u> <u>voice</u>, tells what is being done <u>to</u> the subject of the sentence. The subject is the person or thing that is acting or being acted upon in the sentence. For example:

<u>Active voice</u>: The legislature <u>has passed</u> a law.

<u>Passive voice</u>: A law <u>has been passed</u> by the legislature.

<u>Active voice</u>: Worthington <u>drove</u> the car.

<u>Passive voice</u>: The car <u>was driven</u> by Worthington.

Sometimes writers spend <u>too</u> much time looking for the right verb. Most writers are trained to avoid repeating words in their copy. That may make sense for print, but broadcast writing is conversational, and conversations abound in repetitions of the same word. That's not

7

a license to repeat the same words endlessly, but it is a suggestion not to waste time trying to find substitutes for common words like "say." Certainly it would be bad dialog for all but the most pompous character to say, "I saw the lawyer and he asserted." It would not make much better narrative for your narrator to say, "Many wise men have stated." And it would not make good news copy to write, "The President stated today." In all three instances, "said" does the job.

Sportswriters have been known to invent whole new words to avoid repeating those simple little words "won" and "lost." A certain amount of florid writing is permitted in sports writing, but after a while, a string of substitute words for "won" and "lost" gets to sound far worse than repeating "won" and "lost."

One verb form you should use with caution is the contraction. Words like "haven't," "he's," or "didn't" should be used sparingly. This may seem odd advice because broadcast writing should be conversational--should follow normal speech patterns--and the use of contractions is typical of everyday speech. The problem is that some contractions, especially those ending in "n't," are easily misunderstood. "Have" and "haven't," for example, sound very much alike if you are not listening closely. If there is any chance that the contraction may be misunderstood, write out the complete phrase instead. Broadcast news writers usually carry the rule one step further and underline the "not" or set it off with dots, like this: "The President has. . .not. . .signed the bill." Contractions that cause no confusion, such as "won't," can be used freely.

One aspect of using verbs in broadcasting is primarily a problem of broadcast news writing: the choice of the verb tense used. News writers prefer to avoid using the past tense as much as possible. You may find it necessary in other broadcast writing to cast a story in the present tense or present perfect. Commercials, for example, often use these verb tenses. But in nearly all instances except news writing, the use of these verb tenses follows patterns of normal speech or other kinds of writing. News writers, on the other hand, frequently take stories that would normally be told in the past tense and recast them in the present or present perfect tense. The reason is that the past tense can make news stories sound old and stale. Here are some rules for choice of verbs in news writing. Again, because students may be confused by grammatical terms, we'll explain as we go along.

1. The first choice of verb tense for any news story is the present tense. Try especially hard to keep the first sentence, or "lead," of the story in the present tense. The present tense is the normal verb tense we use for action that is going on right now. When we say "John runs," the verb "runs" is present tense. It tells us what John is doing right now, at this moment. He is running. Note that we have two ways of stating most verbs in the present tense. We can use the verb alone, "John runs," or we can use it with a helping verb, "John is running." Very often when there is no logical way to tell a story in the present tense, it is still possible to find an aspect of the story that is still going on. You can use that aspect for the lead, putting it in present tense, then shifting to past tense when you continue with the story. For example, if the Governor signed a bill this morning, there is no way you can make the signing something that is happening now. But you can find something related to the signing for a present tense lead: "The Governor is declaring war on speeders. This morning he signed. . ." Or you can focus on the consequences of the signing: "It's going to be a lot rougher on people who break the speed limit on the highway. This morning the Governor signed. . ."

2. If there is no logical way to use the present tense, try the present perfect tense. The present perfect tense can be identified

9

by the helping verb "has" or "have," which goes before the verb: "It has rained." "They have left." The present perfect tense tells us that something happened at sometime past, but it does not say when. This is useful to the news writer because the writer tries to keep news copy from sounding dated by avoiding terms like "last night," "yesterday," or "this morning." (This is different from what you may have learned if you have studied print journalism.)

You can easily make use of the present perfect tense in a broadcast news lead. For example, "The Governor has signed a bill increasing penalties for. . ." The writer has avoided having to say when the bill was signed, although that information might come later in the story with a shift to the past tense: "The Governor signed the bill this morning after he. . ."

3. Only when it is clear that neither the present tense nor the present perfect tense will work should you use the past tense for a news story. The past tense is the form of the verb that tells you that the action of the verb has been completed, and it usually requires that you specify when it was completed. That is a distinction between past tense and present perfect that careless writers sometime ignore. A sentence using a verb in the past tense like this sounds incomplete: "It rained." We expect to be told when if a past tense verb is used: "It rained last night." Conversely, it is rarely correct to specify when if the present perfect is used. "It has rained last night" is clearly not good English. Be certain that you do not make this mistake.

EXERCISE 1.1

Make a list of different broadcast writing jobs people hold in your community. Bring your list to class and compare it with the lists prepared by your classmates. (Did anyone have a list that included all the jobs listed by the rest of the class?)

Based on a composite list of all the broadcast writing jobs--plus any the instructor notes the class omitted--the instructor assigns a class member to interview someone in each job category. If possible, take a tape recorder with you to the interview.

Prepare a two-page, typed report on your interview. Be prepared to read your report to the class and discuss it with your classmates. Turn in the report to your instructor after you have reported to the class.

EXERCISE 1.2

Which of the following words would you not use in writing broadcast stories? In each case, write your reasons for not using the word directly beneath the word itself.

1. accessibility

2. alleviate

3. all-round

4. arboretum

5. civility

6. drudgery

7. mesmerize

8. perspective

9. soliloquies

10. stake

11. wholly

12. wrists

EXERCISE 1.3

Improve the following sentences by eliminating excess words, using shorter words, and trimming repeated words. Write directly in the workbook.

1. She went to New York to visit her son John, who is convalescing from an operation for appendicitis, and a daughter.

2. Podunk University has never won a victory over Nevada.

3. Smith, who committed the murder, was never found.

4. On two occasions, my injured knee kept me from participating in the game.

5. The play was under the direction of Bill Jones.

6. He made the statement that. . .

7. The present incumbent is Senator Cranston.

8. It happened all of a sudden.

9. He lifted up the glass.

10. They say Murphy tipped the scales at 300 pounds.

EXERCISE 1.4

Rewrite the following phrases and sentences so they will be examples of good broadcast writing. Write your changes directly in the workbook.

1. a tax on residents

2. His solution was costly and effective.

3. He made the Journey in his truck, carrying with him, since the truck (it had a housedin body with a door at the rear) was new and he did not intend to drive it faster than 15 miles an hour, camping equipment to save hotels.

4. The victim suffered multiple blows on or about the head from a blunt instrument wielded by a person or persons unknown which rendered said victim unconscious and caused multiple bruises and contusions on the head, neck and adjacent parts of the victim's body.

5. The car was driven by Nancy.

EXERCISE 1.5

Brevity and clarity are important to the broadcast writer. You must also write simply and avoid cliches. Here's a list of common cliches that can be written in a shorter, clearer form--many of them in a single word. Find a shorter way to express the meaning of each cliche, writing your answer directly in the workbook.

as luck would have it

at a loss for words

at a tender age

at long last

by leaps and bounds

cut a long story short

few and far between

generous to a fault

hale and hearty

height of absurdity

leave no stone unturned

none the worse

trials and tribulations

EXERCISE 1.6

Little words are the substance of broadcast writing. Change big words in the passages below and see how each sentence becomes clearer. Write directly in the workbook. (A dictionary may be helpful for this exercise.)

1. I discovered the incantation in an arcane, metaphysical tome--one of the antediluvian publications sequestered in the library by my predecessor.

2. Sir, your pettifoggery and obfuscations have only titillated my already insatiable curiosity.

3. In the crepuscular light, I was deluded into thinking it was dawn, and I waited vainly for the Sabbath tintinnabulation from the village churches.

4. Her pulchritude aroused in me amorous sentiments such as I had not encountered since Lydia passed away.

5. The department will facilitate learning experiences by utilizing pedagogical techniques, including extensive practicum, to provide meaningful experiences that ensure the intellectual growth of the student.

EXERCISE 1.7

Shorten the following sentences. (Write directly in the workbook.)
Where a specific noun or verb will do the work of several words, use
it. <u>Hints</u>: Be suspicious of long words, general words, and empty
words. What is the main action in the sentence? Is that expressed
by the verb alone? Cut words that repeat what has already been said.

1. The attorney for the defense appeared on the steps of the court-
    house and told the press that his convicted client was found
    unfairly guilty.

2. A recommendation that the Senate accept the terms of the proposed
    treaty was made by the President in his address to that body.

3. Widespread panic exists throughout the region over the possibility
    that should the river crest over the bank there would be the
    possibility of extensive damage to many homes and the property of
    citizens.

4. Upon reading the side panel, she read that the contents of the
    food included ingredients to which two of the children were both
    allergic.

5. He was discovered as he inadvertently, without intending to,
    moved a branch as he sat in the tree to wait for the enemy
    soldiers to walk beneath his position and be entrapped by his
    sniper's fire.

Your Aunt Minna has written a television script. It has been rejected by every producer she has sent it to. She thinks "maybe it needs a little work on the dialog." (Actually, nothing short of divine intercession will save Aunt Minna's script.) But just to be nice, you agree to look at a short excerpt from the script. On a separate sheet of paper rewrite it so that it is at least simple and under-standable.

JENNIFER

No, Arthur, the relationship between you and me is over and done with. I intend to return to Herbert, in the event that he will have me.

ARTHUR

Herbert! That swart, bourgeoise pedant. Surely you jest! The very thought of such a thing tickles my risibility.

JENNIFER

What is there in the future that I could hope for if I remain with you -- a ménage à trois? You will never take the necessary steps to obtain a legal divorce from your present wife Thelma.

ARTHUR

You understand completely that I have no emotional attachment to Thelma, but she is the victim of a lingering incurable malady from which she will never recover. To leave her would be an unforgivable action.

                         JENNIFER

I am not naive, Arthur. You would obtain

a divorce from Thelma in two shakes of

a lamb's tail if you could retain her

wealth. You are a dastard!

                         ARTHUR

But Herbert is nothing but a tawdry little

poseur -- a fawning parvenu. You cannot

find happiness with such a person.

                         JENNIFER

Oh, Arthur . . .

                         ARTHUR

Yes, ma chérie

                         JENNIFER

Get lost, Arthur!

EXERCISE 1.9

In preparing broadcast news scripts, writers often like to find an
upbeat or humorous story to wind up the show. It helps balance out
the somber note that characterizes most news. Usually these stories,
sometimes called "zippers," are relatively short. The following
fictional story could be a zipper, but it's far too long. On
separate paper, rewrite the story. To conform to typing style of
radio scripts, set your left margin at 10 on the typewriter, and
your right margin at 80. Try to make your story 10 lines long. It
should then take approximately 40 seconds to read.

A cure for the common cold has been found by Oscar Fenton, a
machinist who lives in Phoenix, Arizona. Fenton, who used to work
installing air conditioning equipment in Phoenix homes and businesses,
has developed a device which Fenton says freezes cold germs and
viruses so that they can not give you a cold. Fenton, 38, who lives
at 2735 East 5th Avenue in Phoenix, says his discovery was largely
serendipitous. Fenton says that one day he discovered that his
air conditioning unit at his home was malfunctioning, causing air
passing through it to hit temperatures far below the freezing level
of 32° Fahrenheit (or 0° Celsius, as Fenton prefers to say because it
is more scientific), and then Fenton remembered that no one in his
family had had a cold since the air conditioning was turned on in May.
(It was then July.) Fenton adjusted the air conditioner so that the
air coming out of it into the house through the louvres of the air
conditioning system's duct work was at a comfortable temperature of
about 68° Fahrenheit or 20° Celsius, but so that the air entering the
air conditioner itself was dropped to a temperature of below 32°
Fahrenheit or below 0° Celsius. That was something considerably more
than a whole year ago, and Fenton says he has not suffered a single
solitary cold or attack of the sniffles since he first modified his
air conditioning system that way.

Dr. Ferdinand Toro, a medical doctor who practices medicine in
Phoenix, whom we asked about Oscar Fenton's invention, said he does
not like to be quoted in newspapers, broadcasting or mass media, but
he thinks it is unlikely or at least doubtful that there is much if
any basis for saying with scientific certainty that Fenton's invention
really works and helps keep people from getting colds. On the other
hand, however, Dr. Toro did have some reservations about Fenton's
invention because Dr. Toro fears not only will the invention not work
but it may make things worse by harming people who make use of the
system Fenton invented. Dr. Toro says that when air is made very
cold by reducing its temperature so greatly, the coldness of the air
can be harmful because the chilling of the air removes most or nearly
all of the dampness and moisture in the air. When the moisture is

taken out of the air it becomes extremely dry, and Dr. Toro says dry air can cause irritation or harm to the noses and throats of people who breathe the dry air.

An air conditioning expert, Willis Potlatch, of 18 Sandstorm Road, Sunnyslope, which is a suburb of Phoenix, whom we asked about Oscar Fenton's invention, said that he doesn't know anything about how the invention might help or not help to stop colds, but he says that he does know one thing and that is that if you use Fenton's air conditioning system it will add about $100 a week to your electric bill for air conditioning.

Fenton says what Potlatch says about the cost of running his system is correct, but that it's worth $100 a week to not have to worry about getting a cold.

Script Formats 2

Before you can begin to write broadcast scripts, it is necessary to learn the various formats used for the scripts. There are _five_ basic formats. Each has many variations, but if you learn the basic formats, you can adapt to specific variations as the situation demands.

The five script formats are radio drama, television film, live television, radio news, and television news. Radio drama format is used not only for drama but also for comedy, commercials, and almost any kind of radio writing except news. Television film format is used for videotaped programs as well as those done on film. A program using a live television script format might also wind up on videotape. You cannot always tell from the script format which production techniques will be used.

Don't let this worry you. If a producer is interested in your work, you can obtain sample scripts of the program you want to write for. You can also be reasonably sure that any script that is produced will be typed in final form by members of the producer's staff, who know exactly how the producer wants the script to look. It is unlikely a producer will turn down a _good_ script simply because it was typed in the wrong format.

In this chapter we look at three of the five formats. News formats are discussed in the chapters on radio and television news.

The examples in Figures 2.1, 2.2, and 2.3 contain some terms and abbreviations you may not understand. Don't worry. They will all be explained later in the book.

FIGURE 2.1   Radio Drama Format

"TITLE"

ANNCR: Number pages in the upper right hand corner about an inch from the top and an inch from the right edge of the page. Center the title about two inches from the top of the page. Begin the script about four lines below the title.

NARR: Names of speakers are typed in capital letters about one inch from the left edge of of the page. Dialog for that speaker begins on the same line. Set the left margin for dialog about two inches from the left edge of the page. Set the right margin about one-and-one-half inches from the right edge of the page. Use regular "down style" (ordinary use of upper and lower case letters) for dialog. Radio dialog is usually single-spaced, although some producers use double-spacing because it is easier to read.

Don't indent for paragraphs. Double space instead.

MUSIC: UP FULL, THEN OUT

ANNCR: Write music cues and sound effects in capital letters, starting at the same margin as names of speakers. Underline music and sound cues.

ANY LENGTHY INSTRUCTIONS SHOULD BE TYPED SINGLE-SPACED, IN CAPITALS, BEGINNING AT THE SAME MARGIN AS MUSIC AND SOUND EFFECTS CUES, BUT NOT UNDERLINED.

ANNCR: Such instructions are separated from the
(CONT'D) dialog by double-spacing. If they are long, the name of the speaker may be repeated, followed by the abbreviation "CONT'D" in parentheses. To break a speech between pages, find a logical breaking point and type "MORE" in parentheses, centered about an inch from

(MORE)

ANNCR: the bottom of the page. Begin the second-
(CONT'D) page dialog about one-and-one-half inches
          from the top of the page and always leave
          at least one inch at the bottom of the page.
          Always repeat the name of the speaker, followed
          by "(CONT'D)," if a speech is continued from
          one page to the next. Never split a word
          between pages. While not obligatory in the
          radio drama format, the news-format rules
          which forbid splitting sentences between
          pages and even forbid using hyphens to split
          words between lines are not bad rules to follow
          for dramatic writing as well.

4. NARR It used to be customary to number each new
          speech in a radio script. This is rarely
          done these days. Do not do so unless it
          is requested.

ANNCR: (FILTER) Special microphone effects go in
          capitals with parentheses in the body of the
          dialog. (WITH AUTHORITY) Directions to the
          readers are handled in the same way.

APPLAUSE

MUSIC: THEME UP AND OUT

THE END

FIGURE 2.2   TELEVISION FILM FORMAT

1.

"TITLE"

ACT ONE

SCENE I

FADE IN: 1.

INT. CLASSROOM -- DAY

(THE FIRST LINE OF EACH SCENE SPECIFIES WHETHER THE
SCENE IS AN INTERIOR OR EXTERIOR, WHERE IT TAKES PLACE,
AND WHETHER IT IS DAY OR NIGHT.   THIS IS WRITTEN IN
UNDERLINED CAPITALS, AS ARE THE TITLE, ACT AND SCENE.
SET MARGINS FOR OTHER MATERIAL ABOUT ONE INCH FROM LEFT
PAGE EDGE AND ONE-AND-ONE-HALF INCHES FROM RIGHT PAGE
EDGE.   DESCRIPTIONS OF SET AND ACTION ARE SINGLE SPACED,
CAPITALIZED, AND PUT IN PARENTHESES.)

CU: Blackboard   2.

(FILM SCRIPTS SPECIFY AND NUMBER MOST CAMERA SHOTS.
SET NUMBERS ABOUT ONE INCH FROM LEFT EDGE OF PAGE.
VIDEO-TAPE SCRIPTS SPECIFY ONLY KEY CAMERA SHOTS AND
USUALLY DO NOT NUMBER THEM.)

                          NARRATOR

        Set margins for dialog two inches from

        each page edge.   Double-space, using

        regular lower and upper case letters.

        To continue a speech to a second page,

        type "(MORE)" about an inch from the

        bottom of the page . . .

                          (MORE)

NARRATOR   2.
(CONT'D)   (CONT'D)
(2)

At the top of the next page, repeat the

speaker's name about two inches from

the top, with "CONT'D)" on the next

line, and continue the speech. Names

of all speakers are capitalized and

centered.

Skip an extra line instead of indenting

to indicate paragraphs. (SHORT STAGE

DIRECTIONS MAY BE INSERTED INTO DIALOG,

USING CAPITALS AND PARENTHESES.)

SFX: BELL RINGS

MUSIC: SNEAK THEME

(SOUND EFFECTS AND MUSIC CUES ARE TYPED IN UNDERLINED
CAPITALS, STARTING ONE INCH FROM LEFT EDGE OF PAGE.
TRANSITIONS -- CUTS, FADES, DISSOLVES, ETC. -- ARE
UNDERLINED AND CAPITALIZED. THEY START ABOUT TWO-AND-
ONE-HALF INCHES FROM THE RIGHT EDGE OF THE PAGE, EXCEPT
FOR "FADE IN," WHICH GOES ONE INCH FROM THE LEFT EDGE.
EACH ACT BEGINS WITH A "FADE IN." START EACH NEW SCENE
WITH A NEW PAGE. NUMBER PAGES IN UPPER RIGHT-HAND CORNER.

FADE TO BLACK:

END OF ACT ONE

FIGURE 2.3 LIVE TELEVISION FORMAT

VIDEO	AUDIO	1.
	ACT ONE	
	SCENE I	
FADE IN	(DIVIDE PAGE ONE-THIRD FOR VIDEO, TWO-THIRDS FOR AUDIO. ALL CAMERA DIRECTIONS GO IN THE VIDEO COLUMN, INCLUDING TRANSITIONS. FOLLOW SAME RULES AS TELEVISION FILM FORMAT FOR STAGE DESCRIPTIONS AND DIRECTIONS, EXCEPT THAT LEFT MARGIN NOW STARTS A COUPLE OF SPACES TO THE RIGHT OF THE DIVIDING LINE AND RIGHT MARGIN IS ONLY ABOUT ONE-HALF INCH FROM RIGHT EDGE OF PAGE.)	
LS: Classroom		
SLOW DISSOLVE TO: Blackboard		
ZOOM SLOWLY BACK TO: LS: Classroom		
	NARRATOR	
	Use same margins for dialog as for stage directions. Double-space and use "down style." Treat sound effects and music cues as they are handled in Television-Film Format	
KEY: Slide #1: "Title Page"	MUSIC: STRAUSS WALTZ, SNEAK UNDER.	
	INSTRUCTOR	
	Note camera directions are not	
KEY: Slide #2 "TV Film Format"	underlined. Specify all shots unless told not to. Split speeches between pages as you did in Television-	
KEY CONTINUES	Film Format.	
KEY OUT	Skip a line instead of indenting for a new paragraph.	
FADE TO BLACK	END OF ACT ONE	

Note certain similarities among the three formats. Material not meant to be read aloud is usually capitalized and single-spaced. Copy meant to be read aloud is usually written in normal caps and lower case ("down style") and is double-spaced (although radio drama copy is usually single-spaced). Placement of the copy on the page is designed to keep dialog clearly separated from technical instructions. It's not as strange as it seems. Relax, it will all come to you.

When you send the final version of your script to the producer, you'll want it to be in the right format, to be free of errors, to have all spellings correct, and to have the grammar correct except where intentional errors are used in dialog to delineate a character.

Before the final version of your script is typed, there are certain to be many revisions. You will save yourself time if you learn to edit the rough draft so that it is easy to read. The more changes you can make by editing with a pencil, the less retyping you will have to do.

The rules for editing broadcast copy are simple:

1. Use a soft-lead pencil with a thick point to completely mark out the entire word that contains an error. If you catch the mistake while you are typing the story, you can cross out the word using the "X" key on your typewriter.

2. Type the correction or print it legibly above the material you have marked out.

3. If several words in a row contain errors, mark out the entire row. Do not mark out each word separately.

4. Don't let your corrections turn the copy into a steeplechase for the reader. Don't do this:

The mayor ~~said~~ SAYS he ~~would not~~ WILL...NOT... ask for ~~those~~ THE documents.

The mayor ~~said he would not ask for those~~ SAYS HE WILL...NOT...ASK FOR THE documents.

5.   The final version of your script should be retyped before you submit it.   Even news copy (see Chapters 8 and 9) should be retyped if time permits, and any news copy made difficult to read by editing must be retyped.

Refer to the format models in this chapter when you prepare the chapter exercises, and refer to them regularly as you prepare the rest of the exercises in this book.   You'll be surprised how quickly you learn most of the rules.

EXERCISE 2.1

Reread the instructions for writing a script in television film format. On separate paper that you will hand in to your instructor, write a one-page script using television film format.

EXERCISE 2.2

Reread the instructions for writing a script in radio drama format. On separate paper that you will hand in to your instructor, write a one-page script in correct radio format.

EXERCISE 2.3

Below is a copy of Act I, Scene 1, of Shakespeare's Macbeth. On separate paper that you will hand in to your instructor, prepare it in two formats: (1) as a radio drama and (2) as a television film script. At script's end, indicate the transition to the next scene by a musical bridge for the radio drama and by a dissolve for the television script.

Scotland.   A desert heath.

Thunder and lightning. Enter three Witches.

FIRST WITCH: When shall we three meet again
    In thunder, lightning, or in rain?

SECOND WITCH: When the hurlyburly's done,
    When the battle's lost and won.

THIRD WITCH: That will be ere the set of sun.

FIRST WITCH: Where the place?

SECOND WITCH: Upon the heath.

THIRD WITCH: There to meet with Macbeth.

FIRST WITCH: I come, Graymalkin!

SECOND WITCH: Paddock calls.

THIRD WITCH: Anon.

ALL: Fair is foul, and foul is fair:
    Hover through the fog and filthy air.

                                        Exeunt.

29

EXERCISE 2.5

In rehearsing a radio drama, it becomes evident that you need to cut about 10 seconds of dialog in order to make the program come out on time. You decide the best place to make the cuts is in the section below. Read the material aloud, timing it with a stopwatch. Write the reading time in pencil here _____. Now edit the copy below so that the reading time is exactly 10 seconds less than the time you have written.

NARRATOR: What Galileo discovered when he looked at the moon through his telescope was that the mysterious markings on the face of the moon were mountains, valleys, plains, and craters. The surface of the moon was very much like the surface of the earth!

GALILEO: At first, it seemed so much like the earth that I made some foolish assumptions. I thought some of the broad, dark areas must be oceans like those here on earth.

NARRATOR: The discovery that another body was very much like the earth increased Galileo's conviction that Copernicus had been right.

GALILEO: (MUSING) For if this place we call earth is not so very different from those objects we see in the sky . . . then why should they all revolve around the earth? Couldn't earth too be just another wanderer in space?

NARRATOR: But those were dangerous thoughts.

GALILEO: In 1610, I published a book about what I had seen through my wonderful telescope. Instead of praising me, the Holy Father in Rome issued an edict forbidding anyone to teach Copernicus' theory that the earth revolved around the sun. I became very angry. I even called a cardinal "stupid."

TELEVISION DRAMA 3

Before you begin writing a dramatic script for television, you must
do some spadework. You must learn as much about the program you are
writing for as you can. Not every good script is good for <u>every</u>
program. Here are a few factors that could affect your script.

   1. *Program format*. Is the show a special, a made-for-television
film, or a continuing series? Does it run 30 minutes, 60 minutes, 90
minutes, or longer? Try to watch the show several times--this is easy
with a series, and you should try to tape specials or watch then on
reruns. Time the program with a stopwatch. Learn where program
breaks come and how long each program segment runs. This is very
important in plotting your program.

   2. *Established program themes*. Almost any television series has
some basic theme: a divorced mother trying to make a new life for
herself and her children, a pioneer family facing the dangers of the
frontier, and so on. A program may occasionally depart somewhat from
its basic theme. For example, a detective show may have an episode
that is primarily a comedy rather than a mystery. Nevertheless, a
beginning writer who sticks to the customary theme of the program has
a far better chance of success.

   3. *The characters*. In a continuing series, be sure you study
the main characters of a show carefully before you begin to write

about them. Characters should exhibit the same traits from episode to episode. Occasionally, a show may have a character change in one episode, but in almost all cases the character must revert to "normal" by the end of the show. This is essential in any continuing series because any permanent change will confuse viewers, especially in reruns of the program or when it is syndicated. Stick to the established traits of each character.

4. *Special talents*. In a continuing show, it's best not to write in material that calls for some talent not usually featured such as singing or dancing. Stick to the regularly featured talents of the regular members of the cast. Don't write material that would call for the hiring of a specific actor who is not a member of the cast.

5. *Sets*. If the program is a continuing series, pay attention to the sets on which the action takes place. Don't write material that calls for the construction of special sets or the expense of on-location shooting.

6. *Budget*. Of course you cannot know the exact budget of the program you want to write for, but you should have some idea of production costs. Don't hope to sell a script for a high-budget show to a low-budget program. As an obvious example, don't prepare a script for a student production that would cost $60,000 to produce.

7. *Production techniques*. Your choice of a script format is dictated to some degree by the production techniques used--live, filmed, or videotaped. Far more important than format however, are the limitations the various production techniques place on action. Programs may be produced either before a live audience or on a closed set. If a closed set is used, there is far greater freedom for the placement of cameras, equipment, and performers. A program produced before a live audience may still have some segments produced on a closed set, but generally you will have to restrict the action to one

or two sets and restrict the physical movement of your characters.
If there are no breaks between scenes while such a show is before the
cameras, you may have to write your script so that a character can be
off-camera while moving from one set to another. You might even have
to make it possible for cameras to be out of action while they switch
to the other set.

PLOT AND CHARACTER DEVELOPMENT

In television drama you need to indicate early in the script the kind
of problem that has to be solved. This is complicated by the fact that
the first scenes of the program must also be used to develop the
characters of the key players. Even in a series with continuing
principal actors, an episode may introduce a new character or focus
on a minor character who is less well known to the audience. Some
personality trait of this character often provides the basis of the
plot for the episode. That trait must be established quickly and
clearly at the start of the show.

Character traits can be your plot. Suppose you take as your
basic plot a story about a woman scientist who learns she is dying of
cancer. The whole point of such a story is how a person with certain
traits of character deals with the situation. Suppose she is very
independent. Now she must deal with becoming more and more dependent
as her illness progresses. To make it work, you must establish her
independent nature at the start.

How do you develop the character? You must use every tool at
your disposal to get the point across quickly. To do so, you can
rely on human stereotypes. That you made the scientist a woman
already says something about her character to the audience. Rightly
or wrongly, we attribute some characteristics to men and others to
women. So your choice of the lead character's sex has something to
do with what the audience expects of that character. You can always

reverse stereotypes too. For example, if your lead is a woman, you can make it clear from the start that she does not fit the stereo-type--that she loves baseball and fishing and hates pretty clothes. This serves just as well to define her character, but there is some danger in this technique because audiences have been conditioned to expect characters in reverse-stereotype roles to revert to "normal" at some point in the script. This need not occur in your script, but it is something you must expect the viewers to have in the back of their minds.

The profession you choose for your character helps define the role. Again, we have stereotypes for bankers, football players, college professors, and hundreds of other occupations. Suppose the character we described earlier were not a woman scientist dying of cancer but a male professional football player facing the same fate. The audience would have an entirely different set of expectations about the way the character would face the problem.

If you describe a character as having certain physical traits, that too will evoke sterotyped expectations on the part of the audience. Is the character short, tall, blond, redhaired, fat, thin, black, Oriental, bearded, bald? The character's appearance can suggest character traits to your audience.

Let your plot develop through a series of crises of increasing importance until you reach the final crisis of the program, which should be as near the end of the show as possible. You may find it easier to write the first and last scenes first, then fill in the scenes between. Lay out your plot around the natural breaks in the program for commercials and station breaks. Try to have one crisis resolved shortly before the end of each section and end each section with a new and more threatening crisis facing your leading characters. There are many other ways to approach constructing your plot, but this is a fairly safe route for a writer who is still learning the craft.

TREATMENTS

Usually your plot will wind up as a treatment. This is a written description of the plot. Treatments run about 10 pages. They describe the main scenes of the program, and they include some dialog. They are a bit like a short story. An established writer usually submits only a brief story outline to a producer. The producer then pays the writer to prepare a story treatment. If the producer likes the treatment, the writer is then hired to write the complete script. However, a beginning writer may wish to prepare a fairly detailed treatment as the initial submission to the producer because this will help to demonstrate the writer's skills.

The producer will usually have suggestions for changes in the material you submit. Pay attention to these suggestions. You may not like some of them, but if you want to sell your script, you must be willing to give the producer what he or she wants--at least until you become an established writer.

MINISERIES

A story may be broken into a series of programs. Such miniseries are growing in popularity on television. Basic considerations for writing miniseries are the same as those for writing TV drama, but with mini-series you must give more careful consideration to the structure of your story. Each episode needs to have its own major climax yet maintain the buildup from dramatic peak to dramatic peak within each segment. The ending of each program must set the stage for something more exciting to come so that the audience will tune in for the next episode.

You can achieve some of this by developing subplots and by fleshing out your characters with more action and dialog. You also have the luxury of using a larger number of characters if you wish. Do not overuse this privilege. Remember, you must keep the plot and characters clear to the audience. This is difficult when the story

is broken up over a series of programs. You need not only to summarize previous action at the start of each program but also to make
frequent explanatory references to earlier action in the script to
help your audience follow the plot.

With the miniseries, it is important not only to know where
commercial breaks fall in the individual episodes but also to know
the running time of each episode. Running times may not all be the
same.

DOCUDRAMAS

Docudramas hold a middle ground between drama and documentary.
Research is vital when writing docudrama. You may dramatize events
where the actual facts are not known, but it is ethically dubious to
write material that is contrary to known facts or that introduces
characters or situations that have no basis in history. The basic
freedom the writer of the docudrama has is to introduce, judiciously,
emotional nuances that would be out of place in a true documentary.
It would be foolhardy to substitute your writing for Loncoln's
Gettysburg Address. You can however, introduce stage directions for
the actor playing Lincoln and camera directions that would show the
audience and other speakers reacting to the speech.

The major difficulty with the docudrama is fitting historical
events into a satisfying dramatic structure. This is complicated by
the difficulty of developing character and plot in episodes that may
span considerable lengths of time. Remember that, within reason, you
can use such techniques as the flashback instead of strict chronolog-
ical development to make your story more dramatically satisfying.

SOAP OPERAS

The soap opera can be described as an endless miniseries. You build
within each episode while having each episode end suggesting a more

exciting one to come. Since viewers tune in during the middle of stories and often miss episodes, you must constantly restate themes and repeat names for the audience.

In soap operas you can have an unusually large cast and develop a number of subplots. Indeed, it is difficult to say that a soap opera has one main plot. It has a series of plots running concurrently, some more important than others. The plots must advance slowly so that the viewer does not miss much by missing a few episodes. This means that the characters must do something interesting in each episode, but what they do should not advance the plot much--if at all. Eventually, each problem must be resolved, but the resolution should always take place after new and more complex problems have already been introduced so that the viewer never feels that the crisis has passed. Careful attention must also be paid to the sets that can be used because there is little time or money for building special sets or arranging location shooting.

TECHNICAL TERMS

You need to know the basic terms and abbreviations used in television to write your script. The terms vary somewhat, but the following are in general use in television drama:

FADE IN: The picture gradually appears on a formerly black screen, the traditional opening of a program.

FADE OUT: The screen fades to black; usually the end of a program or scene.

CUT TO: A straight cut from one shot to another, usually used within a scene, but sometimes used as a transition between scenes if change of locale between two shots is clear.

DISSOLVE: First picture grows dimmer as second becomes clearer and replaces first picture. Used to show change of scene, passage of time, or for poetic effects.

WIPE: Picture begins at one edge (usually left) of the screen and moves across it, replacing the picture on the screen. There are *HORIZONTAL WIPE*s and *VERTICAL WIPE*s.

LS: Long shot; any shot wide enough to show a head-to-foot shot of of a character. Needs further description in script.

MS: Medium shot; a shot wide enough to show characters from waist to head.

CU: Close-up; anything showing just head and shoulders.

TCU: Tight close-up; chin to forehead.

XCU: Extreme close-up; focus on a very small area--lips, hands, eyes. Must be spelled out in script.

POV: A shot from the point of view of a specified character.

HIGH ANGLE and *LOW ANGLE:* Normal camera height is about the height of a person's head. **High** and **low** are designated in reference to this and often require some additional description.

PAN: Camera turns in direction specified; similar to turning your head.

TRUCK: Camera physically moves sideways in specified direction; effect is similar to looking out the side window of a moving car.

ARC: Camera makes a circular movement in the direction specified.

DOLLY: Camera physically moves toward (in) or away from (out) subject as specified.

ZOOM: Camera angle is progressively made smaller (in) or wider (out). Effect is similar to *DOLLY*, but camera does not move physically, and movement can be much faster than a dolly.

TILT: Camera is tilted up or down as specified from a fixed position; effect is similar to looking up or down at something from where you are standing.

PEDESTAL: Camera physically moves up or down as specified; effect is similar to looking out of a moving elevator.

CRANE: Used only on high-budget shows. Camera is mounted on a big
crane and can be moved in almost any direction as specified.

EXERCISE 3.1

Team with a classmate and view a television drama while timing it
carefully. Log the times of all important action and all breaks.
Compare notes with your classmate as you work so that you can keep
the times as accurate as possible. Where does the climax of the
show occur? At what points do minor climaxes occur? Can you find
a logical pattern in the placement of these high points? Does the
program build in intensity as it approaches the final climax? What
changes might the writer have made in the script to improve the
structure?

Discuss your conclusions in class, then prepare an outline of
a script you would write for the show. Now, write the scene with
the final climax. Turn the completed work in to your instructor.

EXERCISE 3.2

On a separate sheet of paper that you will turn in to your instructor,
write a page or more of script for one of the following characters,
indicating how you would demonstrate his or her important character
traits to the audience.

Oedipus	Little Orphan Annie
Eliza Doolittle	Superman
Tom Sawyer	Luke Skywalker
Juliet	Madame Bovary
Rip Van Winkle	Mary Worth

Assume that you are doing an adaptation of the works involved. Do
not copy character traits from the original authors.

EXERCISE 3.3

Watch the first five minutes of a television program, and then write in the space provided below a brief prediction of what will happen in the rest of the program. Compare what actually happens with your prediction. Be prepared to discuss the two outcomes in class and to explain what elements in the first few minutes of the show gave you your idea of what would follow.

EXERCISE 3.4

On a separate page, outline a television script. Write the opening sequence so that it foreshadows things to come in the plot. Read it to your classmates and see if they can guess what will happen.

EXERCISE 3.5

Watch a regular dramatic program on television and answer these questions as best you can. Write directly in the workbook.

1. Was this a one-camera or multicamera program? What clues did you use to reach your conclusion?

2. What are the major character traits of the main characters in the program? Are they presented consistently?

3. What means did the writer use to let us know these traits of character?

4. When in the show did the writer introduce these various means of demonstrating character traits?

5. Can you think of ways these traits might have been introduced better or more quickly?

6. Write your version of a scene to introduce a character better than it was done in the original script.

EXERCISE 3.6

List in the space below five examples of foreshadowing that you have seen recently in television dramas. Briefly explain why you think each was either well or poorly handled by the writer.

Write your own version of one of the weak examples, correcting the faults of the original:

EXERCISE 3.7

Pick a regularly appearing television dramatic series, and on separate paper that you will turn in to your instructor, prepare a
treatment of about five pages in length of a story for that program.

EXERCISE 3.8

Prepare a scene, running not more than five pages, for a program
based on the treatment you wrote in Exercise 3.7. Use whichever
format your instructor specifies.

EXERCISE 3.9

Watch a television series with a continuing character. In the space
below, write a brief 250 word description of the continuing character.
Read your description aloud and compare it with the description
written by a classmate.

EXERCISE 3.10

Study a continuing drama on television. On a separate sheet of paper, make notes about the plot. Then write an original plot for the series. Make your plot at least five typed pages in length.

EXERCISE 3.11

On separate paper, outline the plot for a miniseries. The series is to appear in five one-hour episodes, one episode each week. Each one hour program will have six one-minute commercial breaks in it. Here are the time blocks for the show:

:00:30 to :01:00	Open
:01:00 to :02:00	Tease
:02:00 to :04:00	First Commercial Break
:04:00 to :20:00	Act I
:20:00 to :22:00	Second Commercial Break
:22:00 to :37:00	Act II
:37:00 to :39:00	Third Commercial Break
:39:00 to :55:00	Act III
:55:00 to :57:00	Fourth Commercial Break
:57:00 to :59:00	Tag
:59:00 to :59:30	Closing Credits

(In last program of series, tag will be omitted. Act III will run to :57:00, and last commercial break will run from :57:00 to :59:00.)

Outline each episode, indicating the action between each commercial break. Be sure to allow time at the start of all but the first show to recapitulate the action of the earlier shows, and provide a brief tag at the end of all but the last episode to preview what is coming.

EXERCISE 3.12

Prepare a treatment for a one-hour docudrama based on seizure of the American embassy in Tehran, Iran, and the subsequent holding and eventual release of Americans at the embassy. Assume there will be commercial breaks 2 minutes into the story, 20 minutes into the story, 40 minutes into the story, 20 minutes into the story, 40 minutes into the story, and 55 minutes into the story.

Before you begin to write the docudrama, do the following:

1. List the sources you will use for your research.

2. Prepare a chronology of the event, and mark with a check those events in the chronology that you feel should be covered in your script.

3. Prepare a list of the people involved, and mark with a check the ones who should be mentioned in the script.

Now prepare a five-page treatment and turn it in to your instructor.

EXERCISE 3.13

With your instructor's approval, select a soap opera to watch for three weeks. In one-week segments, do the following:

1. Prepare a list of all the major characters in the program during the first week.

2. Write a brief description of the major plot lines and subplots in the program during the first week.

3. Follow the soap opera for a second week. At the end of that week, write a one-page description of what you think the plot of the soap opera will be for the following week.

4. View the program for a third week, and be prepared to discuss in class how closely your predicted plot matched the actual plot of the soap opera.

5. Write a ten-minute scene for the program that would be suitable for the next week's action and turn it in to your instructor.

EXERCISE 3.14

On a separate sheet of paper, prepare an outline for a new soap opera:

1. List and describe the major characters.

2. Describe the locale and major sets to be used.

3. Outline the plot for the first four weeks of the program. Indicate how each program will end, giving particular attention to the Friday programs.

EXERCISE 3.15

In the video column below, write the appropriate cue for the action
described in the audio column. (Admittedly, the action described is
better suited to television film format than live television format,
but this is only an exercise.)

VIDEO	AUDIO
	Program opens.
	Shot of classroom.
	Shot over books on teacher's desk to teacher seated at desk.
	Shot of teacher's head and shoulders.
	Shot of classroom as it appears to the teacher.
	Camera turns left to show window with snow outside.
	Shot of teacher's face. Camera zoom lens narrows in on shot of teacher's eyes.
	Shot of classroom. Child approaches teacher's desk with a paper. Teacher rises.
	Shot with camera placed at height of child so it looks up at teacher.

VIDEO	AUDIO
	Shot of teacher's face as he rises. Camera rises with the teacher so it remains level with his face.
	Shot from teacher's height, looking down at child.
	Camera physically moves slowly left so we see the faces of one child after another in the front row of seats.
	Scene shifts to a shot of a mountain. The camera physically moves toward the mountain until we see a man climbing the mountain.
	Camera starts at base of a steep cliff and slowly tilts upward until it reaches the climber.
	Camera looks down from far above the mountain climber, showing him struggling up the face of a cliff.
	Shot of climber's rope fraying.
	Shot of climber's terrified face.

VIDEO	AUDIO
	Shot from a distance. We see the climber fall.
	The camera slowly circles around the body of the climber on the ground.
	End of Act One.

TELEVISION COMEDY 4

The writing of television comedy is similar in many ways to the writing of television drama. With minor changes, the basic rules outlined for drama can all be applied to comedy. Even the basic premise that the main character must progress through a series of increasingly difficult obstacles to the final solution of the major problem is a typical description of most comedy plots. The difference, of course, is in the <u>way</u> the material is treated. And in comedy, the <u>deus ex machina</u>, or miraculous denouement, is more acceptable. Indeed, it can be very good comedy writing to have the solution to the main problem come from an entirely unexpected source.

A major difference between comedy and drama is that most television comedies are written for the 30-minute format; dramas tend to be 60- or 90-minute shows. The key to writing a half-hour television comedy is the ability to describe action concisely, develop characters quickly through action and dialog, and advance the plot rapidly. Despite the fact that television is a visual medium, comedy writers rely heavily on dialog rather than action.

In the 30-minute weekly series, the problem of character and plot development is difficult. You normally have just a bit over 23 minutes to tell your story. That includes a "tag" at the end, so the actual story has to be wound up in under 23 minutes. The existence

of continuing characters in these series is a godsend to the writer
because they are already known to the audience. You do not have to
explain that this character is cheap, that one smart, and that one
a skirt-chaser. These characteristics are established, and the writer
builds around them, working them into new dramatic situations.

When a new character is introduced to the series or is brought
in for one or two shows, the writer and actor must both work miracles
to help the audience understand the character. This is one reason
that television characters tend to lack subtlety. They must be
understandable to the audience at once, and that means they are often
caricatures.

Dialog, too, must replace action that would take time or cost
too much. In a feature film, you might show an auto wreck. In a
weekly series, someone bursts into the living room and cries: "There's
been a wreck!" In a feature film, you might show a couple walking
home through the park. In a series, they come through the door into
the living room, and the girl says: "Thank you for walking me home,
David. I love walking in the park this time of year."

Details also help build your characters. The accent the actor
uses; whether the character smokes, drinks or chews gum; how the
character dresses--all these things tell the audience what to expect
from him or her. Think about a female character you are developing.
She is to be rich and beautiful. Her dialog may be written as
standard English, and she may sound slightly "cultured." She may
smoke, possibly using a cigarette holder. She may drink, but
certainly not beer. She probably prefers champagne. She does not
chew gum. Television may be faulted for preserving "class" stereotypes, but given the 23-minute format of most shows, the writer would
be hard put to work without them.

The elusive question for every comedy writer is: What's funny?
Obviously, it depends partly on the times in which you write. Scripts

51

written only a few years ago now seem stale, yet we can go all the way back to Aristophanes and find lines that still sound funny. Television writing is a highly circumscribed kind of writing. Your writing must fit the characters who, in most cases, have been created for the show, since most comedy programs are series programs. The producers prefer it if the comedy is not too topical, because topical humor dates programs in reruns or when sold in syndication. Action seems a natural form of humor for television, but because most comedies are shot as three-camera shows, there are heavy limitations on the action you can write for your characters. Added to these restrictions are the fairly extensive codes imposed on television comedy, which make taboo much that might be used in motion pictures or on the stage. No doubt restrictions have loosened, but they still exist. The writer must also be aware that potential sponsors are not good targets for television humor.

Here are a few elements that appear frequently as the basis for television humor:

1. Situations.
   a. Misperceptions, either by one character about another or by both about each other. Example: He mistakes her for the new secretary; she thinks he's an escaped convict.

   b. The imagined predicament. Example: She misunderstands a telegram and thinks she's being evicted.

   c. The misled audience. This follows the same line as a and b, but the audience is not let in on the gag until the end.

   d. Reversed roles. Example: He decides to stay home with the kids; she goes to work at the boiler factory.

   e. Unorthodox viewpoints. Example: The 75-year-old maiden aunt turns out to be a swinger.

g. Funny action. Examples; He strains the spaghetti with a tennis racket; she roller skates in the supermarket.

2. Dialog.

a. Put downs. Example: Basil Fawlty's wonderfully nasty line, "The people in room 14 have never seen chairs before."

b. Retorts. Example: "If you were my kid, I'd poison you." "If you were my father, I'd drink the poison."

c. Analogies and descriptions. Example: "He's got a head like a glass of stale beer."

d. Malapropisms. Example: Norm Crosby's monologue reference to the "uncircumscribed Philistines."

e. Backhanded compliments. Example: "You're as pretty as a plate of hog jowls."

f. Double meanings. Example: Henny Youngman's classic "Take my wife. . .please!"

g. Dialect, which must be used with caution. For example, Fred Allen used to play the character of a Chinese detective Won Long Pan. He would invariably discover a revolver, and in what Allen seemed to think was a Chinese accent, would cry: "A luwalawa!"

h. Word distortion to illustrate character. For example, in the days when there was a Nash automobile, Jim Backus used to play a rich snob who would always "Cadillac" rather than gnash (Nash) his teeth.

i. Spoonerisms. Example: "I fulled my glass too fill."

j. Puns. Example: Haven't you heard of 'mountaineers'?" "No. Have mountain ears heard of me?"

k. Silly rhymes. <u>Example</u>: Gary Moore's old shaggy dog recitation about "Hugh the blue gnu."

3. Satire and parody are beloved by students, but fairly rare because they are hard to do and too transitory for most series programs. Satire spoofs a situation, parody spoofs a style. Both are usually examples of carrying something currently popular to an illogical extreme. Because it <u>is</u> overdone by nature, it is difficult to keep satire and parody from becoming slapstick. It is also increasingly difficult to find something to parody that does not offend some pressure group, and much of today's behavior is so extreme that it is a parody of itself.

4. Nonsequiturs usually have to be combined with twisted logic to make humor. "Why did you hit him with the pie?" "Because it wasn't strawberry." "What's that got to do with it?" "I <u>like</u> strawberry."

5. Unexpected answers. Much humor arises from suprise answers that defy our expectations. For example, in the comedy series "Taxi," the writers stretched a gag based on dialect by adding an unexpected answer. When asked if there were bisexuals in his country, the character Latka Gravas responded that there were many--that people rode around on them and kept them chained to racks at night. When another character explained that Latka meant "bicycles," Latka thwarted the anticipations of the viewers--and got an extra laugh--by saying, "Oh, yes. We have them too."

There are, of course, hundreds of other bases for humor, such as funny sounds, unexpected answers, and old standards like the pratfall and the pie in the face.

Your job is to see to it that funny things continue to happen <u>throughout</u> the show. Humor doesn't just build to one gag; there must be a continual flow of gags or the audience quickly tires. You

need about 20 good gags for one half-hour comedy. Coming up with
that much humor is a tremendous task, which is one reason why comedy
is often written by teams.

EXERCISE 4.1

Watch a currently popular television situation comedy. Time it carefully, using a stopwatch. On a sheet of paper, note the following:

1. The exact amount of time used for each segment of the program—opening theme and credits, opening "teaser" if used, first commercial break, first act, second commercial break, second act, third commercial break, closing "tag" if used, and closing credits.

2. The major theme of the program.

3. Where the key crises arise.

4. When the major problem is solved.

5. When each funny action or line occurs.

In class, compare your data with those compiled by students viewing other situation comedies. (Can you find a pattern that fits most of the programs?) Turn in your time log of the program with a one-page description of the basic format you would use in writing a script for that program.

EXERCISE 4.2

Using the data collected in Exercise 4.1, in the space privided below sketch out the plot line of the first part of a half-hour situation comedy script for the program you viewed. Do not fill in any dialog or jokes, but indicate what occurs in the opening teaser (if the program uses one), how the program opens, what the major theme of the program will be, and how you will end the first act.

EXERCISE 4.3

In the space provided below, write a portion of a scene for the
program you outlined in Exercise 4.2 Indicate where the scene goes
in the plot you have outlined. Use television film script format.

EXERCISE 4.4

In the space provided below, write a portion of a scene that
emphasizes visual comedy. Give a careful description of each piece
of action, and keep dialog to a minimum. Use television film script
format.

EXERCISE 4.5

In the space provided below, write four gags, each using one of the following techiques:

1. Malapropism

2. Non sequitur

3. Misperciption about a character

4. Misperception about a situation

5. A put-down

6. Analogy

7. Backhanded compliment

8. Double meaning

9. Retort

10. Satire or parody.

EXERCISE 4.6

Carefully study the television comedy market, and pick a program you think you can write a good script for. On separate paper, prepare a treatment (4-5 pages) of a script for the show. Remember, the treatment is what sells the script. It should show your best skills in writing and preparing a plot.

EXERCISE 4.7

In the space provided below (add separate pages if needed), write a portion of the closing scene for the show you outlined in Exercise 4.6. Make it as funny as you can, and keep it brief.

EXERCISE 4.8

1. Take notes on an episode of your favorite comedy program. Is there one central problem to be solved by the major characters? Or are there several problems of relatively equal weight?

2. Take the same kind of notes on your second favorite comedy show.

3. Write a one-page essay about each show, summarizing your findings.

4. Be prepared to discuss your conclusions in class.

EXERCISE 4.9

1. Team up with one of your classmates and work together to write a ten-minute comedy script.

2. Turn in your script to your instructor, keeping copies for yourself and your co-author.

3. In class, read some of the gags from this script and a script you wrote alone. Which gets more laughs?

TELEVISION COMMERCIALS 5

and Public Service Announcements

A commercial can be anything from a lavish musical production to an inexpensive "slide with voice over" ad. At its most lavish, the commercial can be the most expensive form of television programming around--on a cost-per-minute basis. But whatever the form or cost, the commercial has one purpose--to sell the product.

That is the point you must always keep in mind when writing a commercial. No matter how artistically satisfying the commercial is, it's a failure if it doesn't <u>sell</u>. Advertising history is filled with sad tales of commercials that everyone liked--but that failed to motivate people to buy the product.

Always begin planning for your television commercial by getting to know the product well. Learn both its good points and its bad ones. If possible, use the product yourself. List the things you like best about the product and those you like least. Then look at the competing products. Try some of them. If you were a user of a competing product, what might make you want to switch to a new brand? What might make you faithful to the old product? If you had never used any brand of that product before, what might make you try using it? What might attract you to one brand over another?

Large corporations and advertising agencies have research staffs that devote all their time to gathering such data and analyzing them for their employers. Because commercials are short--most run for 30 seconds or less--you must focus on one, or at the most two, of the basic appeals you wish to make. There is rarely time to do more effectively.

Your commercial should be keyed to some basic need of the audience, and it should be keyed to the nature of the product. For example, you might stress the quality of a product. In so doing, you are probably appealing to the purchaser's need for self-esteem. The selection of a high-quality product is an individual's way of saying she or he has the intelligence and sophistication to know which products are superior--and the financial ability to own such products. You can key such an appeal to expensive, easily differentiated products, like automobiles. It is not an appeal that would work well with mass-market products, such as chewing gum, or with products that others are unlikely to see the owner using, such as laundry soap, or with products that are too well fixed in the public's mind as lower class products, such as non-premium beer. Manufacturers sometimes wage expensive compaigns to try to change the image of a product. U.S. brewers, for example, have tried for years to give beer more of a "class" image, but the results have not been impressive. Manufacturers also have found ways to differentiate normally indistinguishable products. Examples are neckties by Countess Mara, sports clothes by Lacoste, and various items by Cardin. The manufacturer puts a conspicuous mark on the item of clothing so that the wearer can be sure everyone knows that the tie, shirt, or what-have-you is expensive and presumably of good quality.

The basic needs to which an ad should appeal are fairly easy to define. The difficult part is determining how to appeal to that need. Basic needs can be listed as follows:

1. Security--essentially the ability to control one's own life

instead of being subject to external controls. It implies protection from physical attack and loss of property and protection against hunger and the elements. We all want a warm safe place, good food, and financial security.

2. Sex--broadly, physical appeal to other. The desire for sexual gratification is inborn, and to achieve that gratification one seeks to be sexually attractive. That desire tends to extend far beyond actual desire for sexual contact into a simple desire to be appealing to others, not merely physically, but in terms of personality as well. There is an interaction with the desire for security because from infancy on, we learn that we must be appealing to others to have our needs satisfied.

3. Self-esteem--the need to see ourselves as objects of value. Because we rarely know exactly what others think about us, we rely on our own perceptions of ourselves. These can be at variance with reality. Because reality continually chips away at the false image we carry of ourselves, we need frequent reassurance that we are of some value to others.

4. Variety--we exist in a love-hate relationship with novelty. We feel most secure when we are in the same old rut, yet humans are possessed of a greater sense of curiosity than any other creatures. Can you think of any word that advertisers like to use more than "new"?

5. Play--this may be an aspect of the learning process that grows from our inherent curiosity. Play serves our need for variety and usually involves developing and maintaining a skill. That the skill learned may be of no discernible use in satisfying our other needs seems irrelevant. Indeed, the lack of relation to serving other needs is inherent in the concept of play. Possibly this is simply nature's way of equipping us for future needs we can not foresee. The human desire for "useless" information and play may be what has kept us around so long.

65

THE STORYBOARD

When you are satisfied with the script, prepare a storyboard, sketching in pictures of the key points in the commercial. A storyboard is a device that can be used in almost any form of television production, but its main use today is in the preparation of commercials. Almost no commercial is prepared today without first preparing a storyboard. Simply, the storyboard is just a string of little sketches that show picture and dialog for the main parts of a commercial. It is like a little comic strip, except that the words go below the pictures instead in the balloons within the pictures.

Make a habit of using a story board before you start to write. It will help you visualize your story. You do not have to be a good artist. You can use stick figures, if you must, to sketch out the action. Because commercials are short, storyboards often contain all the dialog of the commercial, with a drawing above each bit of dialog where there is some important visual change. Your storyboard should show each new shot, whether it accompanies a line of dialog or not. You probably will prepare several storyboards for a commercial before you are satisfied. Don't consider that wasted time. It is far easier to correct mistakes in storyboard than it is to have to rewrite an entire script--or reshoot an entire commercial.

POLITICAL ADVERTISING

Political advertising, like all advertising, calls for an analysis of audience and goals and a selection of appropriate needs to which to appeal. It is important to have a clear idea of your purpose at the outset. While most candidates want their advertising to swing votes, it is doubtful that many votes are actually changed by advertising. The major functions of political advertising are to win the uncommitted and keep supporters loyal and active. Well-planned advertising can sustain the momentum in a campaign even when the candidate is running behind (after all, someone has to be behind). This helps

66

maintain the candidate's credibility with the press and prevent defections by supporters to other candidates. If the candidate is ahead, advertising can be used to whip up enthusiasm, win the wavering, and keep the loyal from becoming complacent.

A great deal of political advertising today takes the form of the 30-second spot. Obviously, this limits what can be discussed, but studies indicate that 30-second spots are as effective as longer, more expensive ads. You must be very selective and creative to make full use of these brief messages.

One approach is to appeal to team spirit--to the need for conflict. Make the viewer feel he or she is joining the candidate in battle against the evils represented by the opposition. Stress the groups that have benefited from your candidate and his or her party.

Another approach is to appeal to the need for security. Make the voter feel that your candidate represents safety for the voter-- and that the opposition may be a threat to his or her security.

The copywriter, of course, must defer to the candidate in the major decisions on content, but a good copywriter works hard to make the candidate recognize the realities of television advertising. Despite their popularity, television ads are not magic. Keep your goals simple and realistic.

TELEVISION PUBLIC SERVICE ANNOUNCEMENTS

The Communications Act of 1934 included a provision--Section 307 (c)--that called on the newly established Federal Communications Commission (FCC) to make recommendations to Congress about passing laws that would set aside a specific amount of broadcast time for use by nonprofit organizations. The FCC reported back to Congress that broadcasters were meeting this requirement without legal pressures and that there was no need at that time for laws mandating specific allocations of time to nonprofit groups. In its 1946 Blue Book, the FCC restated the obligation of stations to provide time for such organizations, and that obligation has since been restated in the FCC's 1960 Programming Policy Statement and in numerous other FCC rulings and statements. Stations remain free to determine how much time they will devote to public service announcements (PSAs), when they will schedule those PSAs, and which PSAs they will use. If you are preparing a public service announcement for a commercial television station, you must keep these facts in mind. Your PSA has a better chance of being used if it can be put on the air with minimal effort. Either it should be on film or videotape, or it should provide slides and copy for the announcer to read. Don't expect a station to produce anything more elaborate for you. Since you will probably get a poor time slot for your PSA, be sure you use all your skills as a writer to make the best impression you can on the audience you do reach.

Noncommercial stations cannot run commercials as such, and they sometimes use PSAs to fill in program breaks. The noncommercial station is most likely to choose those PSAs that can be put on with the least effort by the station, and since noncommercial stations usually reach small audiences, you will have to work hard to get the most out of the small audience. So, in some ways, the problems presented in creating a PSA are about the same whether your intended market is a commercial station or a noncommercial one.

Follow the same procedure as for a regular commercial in preparing your script and storyboards. However, prepare three or four different time lengths for each spot. Try to make the same effective combinations of picture and word for each script.

Consider these three versions of a script for an imaginary organization. Note that the shorter versions have been edited down from the longer version. This permits the organization to get three PSAs for about the price of one, since the only work required on the shorter versions is additional film or videotape editing.

68

FIGHT CATHARANTHUS   10 Sec.

VIDEO	AUDIO
	ANNCR
FADE IN: Playing Child	It strikes little children . . .
DISSOLVE TO: Young Mother	It takes the young . . .
DISSOLVE TO: Old Woman	It strikes down the old . . .
FREEZE FRAME: Old Woman SUPER: Catharanthus Logo	Catharanthus . . . With your help, We'll find the cure.
FADE TO BLACK	THE END

FIGHT CATHARANTHUS   20 Sec.

VIDEO	AUDIO
	ANNCR
FADE IN: Playing Child	There is a killer abroad . . . It strikes little children . . .
DISSOLVE TO: Young Mother	It takes the young . . .
DISSOLVE TO: Old Woman	And it strikes down the old . . .
DISSOLVE TO: Scientist in Lab	Catharanthus roseus. Once there was no hope. There still is no cure.

69

ZOOM IN ON: Test Tube FREEZE FRAME	
SUPER: Catharanthus Logo	Support your local Catharanthus Society.
SUPER: Local Address	We'll find the cure.
FADE TO BLACK	THE END

FIGHT CATHARANTHUS   30 Sec.

VIDEO	AUDIO
	ANNCR
FADE IN: Playing Child	This child is in danger. There is a killer abroad . . . It strikes little
DISSOLVE TO: Young Mother	children . . . It takes the young . . .
DISSOLVE TO: Old Woman	It strikes down the old . . .
DISSOLVE TO: Scientist in Lab	Catharanthus roseus. Once there was no hope. There still is no cure.
ZOOM IN ON: Test Tube	But last year, your Catharanthus Society
CUT TO: Scientist FREEZE FRAME SUPER: Catharanthus Logo	supported over two-million dollars worth of medical research to stop this killer.
SUPER: Local Address	Support your local Catharanthus Society
	With your help, we'll find the cure.
FADE TO BLACK	THE END

Less expensive PSAs can be provided with the same three or four-length versions simply by providing scripts and slides that can be used with the scripts. The scripts above could be used with slides instead of as the basis for a videotape. Essentially, all the production techniques outlined in the commercial section can be used for the production of PSAs. There is usually much greater emphasis on the less expensive techniques, however.

WRITING THE SCRIPT

When you have studied your product, organization or candidate and analyzed the competition, select the basic needs to which you can appeal to make your message most effective. Then make two lists for yourself. In one, write down all the ways you can make your appeal with words. In the other, list all the ways you can make the same appeal with pictures. Then try to pick the approach that will make the best use of both sound and pictures.

Write your first draft of the script, paying careful attention to the playing time for each segment of the commercial. Be sure the name of your product or candidate appears in both the sound track and the pictures. Try to use the name of the candidate or the product at least three times. See if you can come up with a clever slogan or visual image for the candidate or the product. Decide whether music will help. (Your instructor can explain the copyright restrictions involving the use of music.) Try to think of some unique device to set your advertising apart in the minds of the public.

Whatever techniques you adopt for your television commercial, each commercial should be a miniature television production. Being shorter doesn't make it easier. If anything, it is more difficult to write successfully within the confines of the commercial's time limits. And however much people may deride them, commercials pay the bills for everything else you see on commercial television. The commercial is a serious form of writing, and to do it well, you must take it seriously.

In the space below, prepare a script for a "straight pitch" commercial
--just the announcer speaking to the camera--no slides, film, video
tape or Chromakey. You may indicate whatever on-camera visuals you
think would help. The commercial should run 28 seconds. The product is
Bic pens. Use live television script format. Use an additional page if
needed. Then prepare a storyboard illustrating the commercial using
the blank sample storyboard on page 74.

74

EXERCISE 5.3

In the space provided below, prepare a simple storyboard for a 30-second commercial. Your product is Glisten, a new fluoride toothpaste that is being introduced to compete with Crest.

EXERCISE 5.4

On a separate page, prepare a commercial script using the storyboard you laid out in Exercise 5.3. Use television film script format.

EXERCISE 5.5

Pick a topic from the list below and write a 10-second PSA to be read voice over a slide. In the space below, sketch what the slide should look like.

1. The American Cancer Society
2. Alcoholics Anonymous
3. The Better Business Bureau
4. Little League
5. National Association for the Advancement of Colored People

EXERCISE 5.6

In the space provided below, prepare a 20-second PSA script to warn
viewers of the dangers of walking across streets against the stop-
light or not using the crosswalk. Use any technique and script
format you wish.

EXERCISE 5.7

In the space provided below, rewrite the PSA you prepared in Exercise 5.6 as a 10-second PSA.

EXERCISE 5.8

In the space provided below (use extra paper if necessary), write a 30-second commercial for a brand-name product or a political advertisement for a candidate running for local office.

EXERCISE 5.9

On a separate sheet of paper, write a one-minute PSA for the American Cancer Society. Prepare it so that it can be edited down into 30-second, 20-second, and 10-second versions. (Reread the "Fight Euphorbia" PSA at the end of the chapter.) Underline material you would cut for the 20-second version with one line. Underline material you would cut for the 10-second version with 2 lines.

EXERCISE 5.10

Have your instructor pick two candidates for the same office or a major ballot issue in an upcoming election. The election can be national, state, county (or parish), city, or campus. (If there are no elections coming up, the instructor can select an issue or candidate likely to be on the ballot in the next election.) The instructor can divide the class into two teams, one for each candidate or each side of the issue. Each team must map out a television advertising campaign for the election. Every member of each team writes one 30-second commercial for his or her side in the election.

Use any technique you think will work well. Turn in your script to your instructor with a brief explanation of the particular basic needs to which you were appealing.

Later, in class, the two teams compare campaigns. If elections were decided by television advertising, which side would have won the election? Why?

and Comedy

Once among the most popular forms of American entertainment, radio drama and comedy have been declared as dead as the dodo by some in recent years. A quick look (or listen) proves that this is not so. The two radio forms have adapted to the times and are very much with us.

RADIO DRAMA
The only regularly scheduled network drama now on commercial radio is "CBS Mystery Theater." A number of syndicated dramas are carried by commercial stations around the nation; the Salvation Army's "Heartbeat Theater" is one of the better-known of these dramas. There has also been an upsurge in old radio programs, with both commercial and noncommercial stations airing network and syndicated shows that went off the air years ago. Meanwhile, public radio has provided both network and local dramas. Notable PBS series include "Earplay," "Star Wars," and "Masterpiece Radio Theater."

    While network and syndicated programs are a difficult market for the beginning writer to crack, many excellent local programs are on college and other noncommercial stations, and these provide opportunities for writers who have not yet established their reputations. A few organizations, such as American Radio Theater in

Glendale, California, hold contests for radio drama scripts.

For writer, performer, and audience, radio drama remains one of the most stimulating forms of drama to work in. No other medium allows so much latitude for creativity.

The construction of the radio drama follows the same basic pattern described in the section on television drama. The main character must pass through a series of increasingly difficult obstacles, each seeming to put the hero or heroine farther from the goal. The major obstacle is faced near the end of the program, followed by a very quick denouement.

Keep the number of characters smaller than you would for television. Each character has to be identified by his or her voice, and the listener cannot be expected to distinguish more than a few voices without difficulty. Names of characters should be repeated frequently to help the audience recall which voice is which. Pay particular attention to speech patterns of different characters, using these in addition to grammar and dialect to help distinguish characters. (Be careful not to use dialects that people may find offensive or demeaning.)

Don't write words that are difficult to pronounce for your characters, and make sure that there is no ambiguity about the meaning of the words you write (unless such ambiguity is the point of the story). Take this sentence: "She was sure she wouldn't finish the dress. I told her, 'Sew!'" The audience might mistake that last phrase as "I told her so."

Dialog should fit the characters speech patterns, but it will be easier for your actors if you keep the sentence structure relatively short and simple.

You probably will find a greater need for a narrator in radio drama than in television writing. You may have a formal narrator who is "outside" the drama itself, or one of the characters in the drama may "tell the story." However, you can usually tell most of

the story with careful use of dialog. For example here are two ways
of handling the same opening sequence:

NARRATOR: They call the grave a final resting place. If
          so, a graveyard should be a restful place. . .
          especially at midnight. And the two men, one
          young, the other old, who entered this graveyard
          in the English moors . . . surely a peaceful
          place . . . ought to have found it restful
          indeed on that night in 1871.

Here the narrator carried the burden of setting the scene. It could
have been done this way:

FADE IN.

SOUNDS OF WIND. A DOG HOWLS. THEN THE SOUND OF THUNDER
AND A BELL BEGINS TO STRIKE TWELVE.

KORF: Listen to that! It's midnight already!

FINN: (CACKLES) Don't tell me, young gentleman, that
          you're afraid to be in a churchyard at midnight.

THUNDER

KORF: Of course I'm not, you half-witted old fool.
          But if you'd hurried up we'd be home by now.
          It's going to pour down any second.

FINN: Young gentleman doesn't like our weather out here
          in the moors. He'd rather be home in London,
          heh?

KORF: I'd rather be in one of these graves than stuck
          out here with you. . . . Hey . . . Look! Here
          it is. This is the one.

THUNDER

FINN: (READING) "Edward Martin Crandall. Born
          April 8th, 1802. Died August 29th, 1871."
          (REPEATING) August, 1871. . . You ain't give
          him much time to cool down, have you? That's
          less than a month ago.

Both versions introduce the same material to the audience, but in very different ways. Both paint a picture of the scene. The narrator version obviously covers the material more quickly than the dialog. On the other hand, the dialog gets us into the action of the story more quickly. Which technique you choose depends on personal preference and the amount of time you have to tell the story.

Be sure that in plotting your story you pay close attention to the points at which you must break for a commercial. Just before a commercial break is a good place to introduce a new crisis so that your audience is anxiously waiting to find out what happens after the commercial. Be sure there is a clear indication of the ending of each segment. Remember, the audience has no visual cues to indicate when the story has been interrupted and the commercial begun. Again, a host or narrator can provide the transition. Or it can be done by fading out a musical theme or with some similar device.

RADIO COMEDY

Before you write a comedy program, determine which format you intend to use. Will the program be essentially episodic, or will it be one unified, humorous story? If it is episodic, will it function within the framework of a story, or will it be a series of acts, as in a revue?

Sketch out the basic story line or the sequence in which you will present the segments of your revue. Then determine who the important characters are and what image you must create for each character to identify that character for the audience. Consider what methods you can use to create an image. You can indicate things by the way the character speaks. You can have other characters describe a character. You can give characters lines that delineate their idiosyncrasies. You must do all you can to get key characters established as individuals at the outset.

Block out each segment of the show, including what you think will be the funniest lines in each segment. Use sound freely as another source of humor along with words. Now, begin to fill in the rest of the dialog, segment by segment. Try to hold the funniest lines until near the end of the segments so that each scene builds and you can obey the old show business maxim "Always leave 'em laughing."

Now make a rough time check of the script and see where you need more material and where you need to tighten. Some old comedy programs managed to work in four or five funny lines per minute, with stretches where gags came only eight or nine seconds apart. Naturally, in some places the gags were more widely separated, with some punch lines taking more time to set up. The trick to such fast-paced comedy is finding little gags that can be the buildup for major gags. You can use malapropisms, dialect, funny sounds, and similar techniques to provide little laughs between the big ones.

Go over your script and check those places where there is more than ten seconds between funny lines. See if you can't fill some of the gaps with new jokes. Sometimes it helps to run through the lines with friends. Often, where comedy is concerned, the more writers, the merrier the script.

When you have completed the script and crammed as many jokes into it as you can think up, put it aside for a few days. Then read it over again aloud, timing with a stopwatch. Better yet, have a friend read it aloud while you listen and time it.

There are two extremes you must avoid in writing comedy. One is becoming so enamored of your own jokes that you fail to eliminate the weak ones. Never stop looking for a funnier line than the one you have. The other extreme is to become disenchanted with what you have written. After all, you have been working with it for a long time. No wonder some of the jokes no longer seem funny to you. Writers have been known to throw out very good material simply because they could no longer believe it was funny. Often you need a fresh opinion on something like this. If you thought a gag was great once, and now have begun to have doubts, try it out on a couple of people who haven't heard it before and see how they react.

Finally, it is important for the writer to work with the cast when they begin rehearsing the script. Often a funny line simply won't work with the actor assigned to read it. Be ready to rewrite lines, or reassign them to other characters. Moreover, in the rehearsals, when the script really begins to come alive, new ideas for lines are sure to crop up--and old ones are bound to prove unworkable. These last-minute revisions can do much to improve a comedy. Often those little gags you couldn't think of to fill in the dry spots will pop up.

It's a cliche, but bitterly true--there's nothing funny about comedy. Writing comedy is one of the hardest jobs a writer can undertake. There is a great deal of difference between being a witty person and being someone who can turn out a hundred gags for a half-hour show. It is a craft that must be learned and practiced to be done well. But it is not a trivial craft. It is one you can practice with satisfaction. Think for a moment about the programs writers recall from the Golden Age of Radio. What the critics and the ordinary people alike remember are the comedies.

EXERCISE 6.1

Using an audio tape recorder, tape the sound track of a television
drama. In the space provided below, outline the plot, noting times
for breaks and placement of key action. Now listen to the tape
again and note every place where you would have to make a change in
the script to make the story work as a radio drama.

EXERCISE 6.2

Pick one of the following and script enough of the scene to show how
you would present the material without narrative, using only dialog
and sound effects. Do the scene on pages that you will turn in to
your instructor.

1. Late one foggy night, a sailor with a wooden leg meets a friend
    on the docks and begins to plot a murder.

2. An old woman looks into a mirror and sees the ghost of her long-
    dead lover standing behind her. Her maid sees nothing.

3. A Confederate soldier trying to infiltrate a Union camp by night
    is halted by a Union sentry. They grapple for the sentry's
    rifle. It goes off, and the sentry is killed.

4. A cowboy, galloping his horse at full speed to head off a
    stampede, is thrown when the horse stumbles. The cowboy falls
    in the path of the stampeding herd, but is saved at the last
    minute by a mysterious stranger who rides in, shouting and firing
    his pistol, and heads the herd in another direction.

5. The head of a supersecret atomic testing laboratory is discovered
    to be a spy from the Planet Xenon. He has killed the real head
    of the laboratory and taken over his body. When confronted, he
    paralyzes his accusers with a ray gun and then disappears into
    thin air.

EXERCISE 6.3

In the space provided below, script a short radio story that uses only sound effects. Length is unimportant. See how much you can do with sound and music and no dialog.

Indicate which transitional devices you would use to go from one scene to the next in each of the following situations:

1. A man finds a magic talisman and, by its use, is transported from the present to Paris in the time of Napoleon.

2. A woman falls asleep in her bed and dreams she is in a tomb.

3. As one scene ends, we find the hero on shipboard in a violent gale. The next scene presents his wife, waiting in their seacoast home, worrying about her husband.

4. We go from a conversation between two people to the actual thoughts of one of them.

5. The old movie "cut-back." We go from the heroine, whose life is being threatened by the villain, to the hero, who is rushing to her aid, then back to the heroine.

6. Indicate the passage of three hours' time for two people waiting in a darkened room for someone to force an entry into the room to retrieve an item and thereby indicate that he or she is the mysterious murderer they have set out to trap.

EXERCISE 6.5

Every writer must know her or his audience. Prepare two radio
comedy skits, each running two minutes. Aim each skit at a different
radio audience. Indicate the radio station and the time of day you
would want to present each skit. Suggest possible sponsors for each.
Turn in your skits to your instructor.

EXERCISE 6.6

In the space provided below, outline a 15-minute radio drama you
intend to write. Plan a 30-second commercial break one minute into
the program. Plan a 60-second commercial break 7 minutes into the
program. Plan a 30-second commercial break 13 minutes into the
program. Indicate in the outline where the key elements of action
will occur.

EXERCISE 6.7

In the space provided below, list every speaking part in the program
you planned in Exercise 6.6. Write a one-paragraph description of
the way you visualize a leading character. Explain what techniques
you will use to help the audience visualize that character.

EXERCISE 6.8

In the space provided below, write a short radio comedy skit in which at least some gags depend on humorous sound effects.

EXERCISE 6.9

Many contemporary radio comedians incorporate references to their
sponsors into their shows. This can be risky. It is all right to
provide a humorous lead-in to a commercial; it is _not_ all right to
make fun of the product--unless you have a special agreement with
the sponsor. On separate paper, prepare a 5-minute comedy show that
contains two 30-second commercials. Integrate the commercials into
the show so that they are introduced in a lighthearted way but do
not make fun of the product. You may use two commercials provided
by your instructor, or if the instructor prefers, use Wrigley's
Doublemint Gum and Adidas athletic shoes as the sponsors.

EXERCISE 6.10

Pick one of the following topics. Get the book on which the scene
is based, and read through the author's description carefully. On
separate paper, prepare a five-minute adaptation of one of these
scenes. Turn in your adaptation to your instructor.

1. Raskolnikov says good-bye to his mother before going to confess
    his crime to the police. Dostoyevsky, Crime and Punishment.

2. Scarlett and Rhett's daughter Bonnie dies in a riding accident.
    Mitchell, Gone With the Wind.

3. Ben Gant's death. Wolfe, Look Homeward, Angel.

4. Yurovsky and his henchmen murder the tsar and his family.
    Massie, Nicholas and Alexandra.

5. Senators Scott and Goldwater and Congressman Rhodes meet with
    President Nixon to get the President's final agreement to resign.
    Woodward and Bernstein, The Final Days.

EXERCISE 6.11

Listen to a radio drama. In the space provided below, note the number of people in the cast; the differences in the voices of the cast members; the number of times the writer has used each character's name in the dialog; the number of minutes the narrator speaks, if one is used; any problems you encountered in understanding what any character said.

RADIO COMMERCIALS 7

and Public Service Announcements

When you write a radio commercial, you are appealing to the same basic needs discussed in the chapter on television commercials. The important difference, obviously, is the lack of a visual dimension. The pictures in a television commercial do much to reach the inner needs through which the commercial conveys its message. But the difference, where radio commercials are concerned, is just that--a difference--not a disadvantage. True, you cannot <u>show</u> the images you desire, but you can <u>create</u> those images in the imagination of the listener--and they can be even more effective than the ones shown on television--because each image fits the personal preconceptions of the viewer who created it.

Of considerable importance is whether the commercial is to be prerecorded and distributed on discs or audiotape, or whether it will be prepared in script form only to be read by local announcers. Obviously there is greater control over production of the commercial in the first instance. On the other hand, the script-only commercial is cheap and easy to distribute. Some feel it also has the advantage of being presented in a voice familiar to the listener.

The script-only commercial generally has to be a "straight pitch." It provides a message read directly to the listener, with no attempt to dramatize or use gimmicks to catch and hold the listener's attention. A typical script-only or "reader" commercial might look like this:

HELEN'S FLOWERS   30 Sec.

ANNCR: Got a special event coming up? There's no nicer way to
          show that you remembered than with a corsage or bouquet
          from Helen's Flowers. Helen's. . .at the corner of Oak
          and Main in downtown Wemberly. . .is open 'til nine every
          week night. This week Helen's has a special. . .just in
          time for those June anniversaries. . .one dozen long-
          stemmed red roses for just fifteen dollars. They're the
          one gift everyone can enjoy. That's at Helen's Flowers,
          corner of Oak and Main in downtown Wemberly.

Here the need being addressed is sex, but not necessarily in the carnal sense. It urges you to show someone you like them and want to be liked by them in return, all through giving a gift. The name of the store is mentioned three times, the location twice. The naming of the city in which the shop is located is important for most stations, since radio signals usually carry over a considerable distance. There could easily be more than one community in the station's area of coverage that has a "corner of Oak and Main."

Far more interesting, usually, are commercials that are pre-packaged and distributed to the stations on which time has been bought. Here much greater attention can be given to production details. The commercial may still be only a "reader," but now a musical background can be added or perhaps sound effects.

More elaborate commercials are really little radio dramas or comedies. The difficulty faced in preparing these little comedies or dramas is to introduce characters, set locales, and establish situations in one minute or less. The cliche is of great value to the copywriter here. For example, most of the 27 commercials done by Jerry Stiller and Anne Meara for Blue Nun Wine presented the same

97

stock characters in slightly different guises. Stiller was always
the long-suffering male, Meara the not-too-bright lady--a kind of
update of the material George Burns and Gracie Allen did in earlier
years of radio, or perhaps Goodman Ace and his wife, Jane. The
point is that the audience knew what to expect from each character,
so no particular effort had to be expended in developing the
characters. When Stiller explained that he had just brought "a
little Blue Nun home for dinner," the audience was ready for Meara
to say, "No wonder she's blue, it's freezing out there."

Most of the material you prepare as a student will not have
that advantage. The audience will not know the characters you
introduce, and you will not have one of the top comedy teams in the
country to perform your script. So plan your work accordingly--to
scale, so to speak.

You can establish characters quickly in this brief format either
by identifying them as some character the audience already knows or
by immediately introducing some distinguishing characteristics in
the dialog.

Here is how you might use a known character to quickly establish
the main character in your commercial.

XTRACHROME TAPE   30 Sec.

MUSIC: MOONLIGHT SONATA, UP AND UNDER.

ANNCR: Uh . . . Herr Beethoven . . . pardon me.

MUSIC STOPS SUDDENLY.

BEET: Vat's dat? You gotta talk louder, please.
           Dot's my bad ear.

ANNCR: Sorry. We were just wondering what the world's
           greatest composer thinks of Nagagami's new
           Xtrachrome Recording Tape.

Here's how you can use dialog to establish characteristics.

MURPHEY'S JEANS   1 Min.

ELIOT: (WHINING) Take them back, Martha.

MARTHA: But, Eliot, they're Murphey's Jeans.

ELIOT: I'm not a kid, Martha.

MARTHA: Murphey's Jeans aren't just for kids, Eliot.

ELIOT: Take them back, Martha. Grown men don't wear jeans.

MARTHA: But Murphey's are cut to fit grown men. And they're so comfortable to wear . . . well . . . you'll feel like a kid again. . . .

In each example we learn what the characters in the commercial are like after only a few seconds of dialog. With the characters and situations established, you can begin developing your main theme --your sales pitch. If you have used a dramatized situation, you must allow some time at the end of the commercial for the denouement of the situation you have created. If the situation is a humorous one, then you should try to end the commercial on a light note. If the message is serious, the final lines should show how the product has solved the problem. For example:

MARY: Feeling better now?

JOHN: My headache is all gone. The next time I've got a headache, I'll remember Aspir-Fizz.

ANNCR: Aspir-Fizz! . . . when your headache won't go away. . . . Available at drugstores everywhere. . . . Take only as directed.

THE END

Or, to wind up a humorous commercial:

ELIOT: You're right, Martha, these <u>Murphey's Jeans</u> do
            make me feel like a kid again.

MARTHA: <u>Murphey's</u> are for adults, Eliot, not kids.

ELIOT: Martha? . . .

MARTHA: Yes? . . .

ELIOT: Can I have an electric train?

MARTHA: No, Eliot!

ELIOT: Gee whiz, Martha! All the other stockbrokers in
            my office have one.

MARTHA: No, Eliot!

<u>BEGIN FADING SOUND OUT SLOWLY.</u>

ELIOT: But I feel like a kid!

MARTHA: No, Eliot!

<u>UP FULL</u>

ANNCR: <u>Murphey's</u> . . . the jeans for adults . . . well
            . . . mostly for adults. . . . At better
            department stores everywhere.

<u>THE END</u>

RADIO PUBLIC SERVICE ANNOUNCEMENTS

The public service announcement is an advertisement. For radio as
for television, it should be prepared with the same care that you
would give to an ad for a product. You should analyze the message
you are trying to get across just as you would analyze a product you
are trying to sell. What is there that is particularly appealing
about this cause? (Remember, you are already convinced. Ask
yourself what someone not well acquainted with the organization
would find appealing.) What is <u>not</u> appealing about the cause you

are advocating? Look hard at this point. Even the most popular
organizations have their weak points. Then ask yourself what human
need you can appeal to. Don't try to frighten the audience into
supporting your cause, and don't promise results that are not likely
to be achieved.

You should not expect that an appeal that works on a Top-40
station will work on a station that plays religious music. Indeed,
a major reason given by stations for rejecting PSAs is that the
message does not fit the station's format.

Listen to any station you intend to send a PSA to. Tailor your
PSA to the format of that station. Pay particular attention to the
product commercials used on that station. Some locally produced
commercials may show no better planning than poorly placed PSAs,
but most spot announcements produced and placed by national advertising organizations are created with great care, designed for the
specific audience that listens to that station. Aim your PSA for
that same audience.

Oddly enough, a major objection cited in one servey of radio
usage of PSAs was the use of loud rock music as a background for the
message. Given that Top-40 is one of the most used formats in U.S.
radio, it would seem that rock music would work well--but most
stations serveyed said no.

As with the television PSA, it is best to produce a radio PSA
in a variety of time formats. Studies indicate that the format most
likely to be used is the 30-second spot. But it is a good idea to
provide the station with alternatives to fit specific time require-
ments. Another complaint cited by stations is that PSAs often are
inaccurately timed. Be sure that your script is timed precisely.

To review: Study the strong and weak points of the organization
you are promoting. Give your message a positive, nonthreatening
tone, but not one that promises miracles. Study each station you
intend to send the PSA to. Design your message to reach the

audience of that station. Don't forget that <u>any</u> radio spot must be interesting and entertaining. And pay very close attention to the timing of your spots. Stations sell time by the second. Don't expect them to pay less attention to those seconds when they are giving them away.

EXERCISE 7.1

In the space provided below, prepare a 30-second commercial script to be read by a local announcer for a brand-name product. The material must be timed <u>precisely</u>. The station for which the commercial is being prepared is a Top-40 format station.

EXERCISE 7.2

Whisk is a new brand of razor blade. It comes in sizes to fit all razors. Its main sales angle is that it is made of a new "space-age ceramic, which was developed for America's space-exploration program." Ceramic blades are reputedly stronger than steel and have a smooth, slippery surface that slides over the skin more easily than metal blades. The manufacturer had wanted to claim that the blades were sharper than steel blades, but the Federal Trade Commission found no significant difference in the sharpness of the ceramic blades and good-quality steel blades. You have been advised by the FTC not to make any claim that the blades are sharper than steel blades. The blades have been priced at about 10 cents more than the most expensive metal blades for a package of 5 blades.

On separate pages that you will turn in to your instructor, write a brief but well-thought-out description of the audience you are trying to reach. Make a list of the station program formats you want to use to reach your audience. Then write a 60-second drama-tized commercial for Whisk razor blades. You may use either a serious or humorous approach.

EXERCISE 7.3

The makers of Whisk razor blades would also like to sell their product in the lucrative women's market. Marketing research indicates that the best approach is to market a new razor for women rather than just selling blades. (It had earlier been decided to offer men the new blades for use in existing razors.)

The manufacturers have designed Lady Whisk, a lightweight, plastic razor that uses one of the regular sizes of Whisk blades. The new razor's shape is slightly different from that of a man's razor, and the razor is somewhat smaller and lighter than most men's razors. The plastic has been dressed up with metallic trim to make the razor look more elegant. To push the "class" image, the manu-facturers have arranged to have the razor introduced in a "leather-look" case designed by the expensive Italian leathergoods firm, Gucci. The razor is being introduced at a high price to promote the "class" image. Initial selling price for the razor in the Gucci box, with five razor blades, has been pegged at $7.95. Later the manu-facturer plans to introduce a less fancy model at $4.95, and then a mass market model for $2.95.

On separate pages that you will turn in to your instructor, describe the audience you are trying to reach and the types of radio stations you would use to reach it. Then prepare a 60-second dramatized commercial for the product. Do you think a humorous commercial would be appropriate for this ad?

EXERCISE 7.4

In the space provided below, outline a 30-second version of the commercial you wrote for Exercise 7.3.

EXERCISE 7.5

Pick a local business that could benefit by advertising on the radio. Plan a series of three or four ads for that business. In the space provided below, briefly outline what the content of one of the advertisements would be. Describe the audience you are trying to reach and the stations you would use to reach that audience. Specify the times of day you would want the ads to run and some of the programs you would want the ads to run on. Then prepare a 30-second commercial, using any format you wish, to be the first commercial in the series.

EXERCISE 7.6

Pick any two of the following stations: WBBM (AM), KFSG (FM), KALI (AM), KQIZ (AM), WSKE (AM), KUSC (FM). Check their location, format, and market size in the latest edition of Broadcasting Yearbook or a similar publication. On separate pages that you will turn in to your instructors, prepare a 30-second public service announcement for each of the two stations you selected on this topic: The National Safety Council wants to warn people to drive safely over the upcoming Thanksgiving weekend.

EXERCISE 7.7

Based on your study of the various station formats in your area in Exercise 7.6, in the space provided below list for each of the following PSAs which stations would be the most effective in getting your message across and which would be the least effective.

1. An American Lung Association announcement telling people where they can obtain free chest X rays.

2. An American Cancer society appeal for all women over age 40 to get a Pap test.

3. An American Heart Association appeal for people to reduce the amount of food they eat with high cholesterol content.

4. An appeal by the County Health Department for all children of school age to be vaccinated against a new strain of influenza.

5. An appeal by the Red Cross for canned food and warm clothing to help victims of a flood in the next county.

6. Announcement by the city bus lines of a new, lower fare for people over 65 years old.

7. An appeal for funds to support black colleges and universities.

8. A city school system announcement of special free English courses for people who do not speak English.

9. A reminder to property owners that county property taxes are due at the end of this month.

10. A recruiting ad for the U.S. Marine Corps.

EXERCISE 7.8

Pick one of your local radio stations. In the space provided below,
prepare a 10-second PSA for that station on this topic: Your city's
Suicide Prevention Center has a hot-line number people can call if
they feel depressed, suicidal, or in need of help. The number is
555-0020. The center is open 24 hours a day, 7 days a week.

EXERCISE 7.9

The Salvation Army in your community is seeking food, clothing, and donations for the needy. The drive is scheduled to coincide with the Christmas holidays--with Christmas now only two weeks away. On separate pages that you will turn in to your instructor, prepare a 30-second PSA for a local Top-40 station and then a 60-second PSA for a local noncommercial, college station.

EXERCISE 7.10

Pick a charity or cause that interests you. In the space provided below, prepare a 20-second PSA for that charity. List the stations for which you think your PSA would be appropriate.

EXERCISE 7.11

On separate pages that you will turn in to your instructor, write a
PSA on the benefits of not smoking. Prepare it in 10-, 20-, and
30-second versions.

EXERCISE 7.12

Pick a product sold locally. In the space provided below, write a
humorous 30-second commercial for the product.

Writing

News writing calls for very different techniques from the ones you have learned for other forms of broadcast writing. If you have studied print journalism, you will find that broadcast journalism techniques also differ from those of print. We can give only the briefest summary here of the major differences. The Broadcast Writing textbook contains a more complete summary of the rules for writing broadcast news.

Brevity is the essence of broadcast news writing. Strip your story to the essential facts. The audience cannot remember details. Remember, most radio news "readers" (stories with no audio cuts in them), run only 20 to 40 seconds. Even stories with audio cuts seldom run as long as one minute. Don't write fact-crammed newspaper leads. Don't try to tell "who, what, why, where, when, and how." Keep details and important facts out of the lead. Use the lead to tell the audience what the story is about, and let the facts come in the body of the story. Don't put unfamiliar names in a lead. Keep numbers out of leads. For example:

Poor:

Twelve-hundred members of Teamsters Local 795 spend 6 hours in 90 degree heat today at Teamster Headquarters, 792 South 25th Street, Carbondale, listening to Local Chairman Peter L. Fong, 35, urge them to accept the offer of the United Truckers Association of Carbondale for a wage and benefits package of 7 dollars and 12 cents the first year, 6 dollars and 92 cents the second year, and 5 dollars and 22 cents the third year.

Better;

Members of the Teamsters Union are considering the latest offer from Carbondale truckers.

Never lead with a quote, and avoid quotes elsewhere in broadcast writing. Paraphrase quotations whenever possible. Always put the source of a quote or other information before the statement, not after, as is done in newspaper writing. For example:

Bad:

Drinking water from the city water mains can lead to insanity, sterility, and even death, according to members of a religious sect that teaches indoor plumbing is a work of the devil.

Better:

A local religious group wants people to stop using indoor plumbing.

Stories should be timed with a stopwatch, although you can estimate reading time while writing by keeping track of the line count. If you set your typewriter margins at 10 and 80, each line should take about four seconds to read. Write the reading time or line count for each story in the upper-right-hand corner of the first page. Include in the reading time or line count the running time of any recorded material in the story. For example, a story with six-teen seconds of written copy follwed by recorded audio running twenty seconds should have either ":36" or "9 lines" written in the upper-right-hand corner. Page numbers are written in the upper-left-hand corner. Pages are numbered only after the final version of the script has been assembled.

Each story has a "slug," or title, at the tip of the page. It contains the name of the story, the program for which it is written, the date, and the name of the writer. It may be written in capital letters in a single line across the top of the page:

FEDERAL BUDGET -- NPR MORNING EDITION -- 10/27/84 -- GONZALES

or it may be written in a four-line block in the upper-left-hand corner, below the page number, like this:

Federal Budget
NPR Morning Edition
10/27/84
Gonzales

Double- or triple-space your copy. Use regular capital and lower-case letters ("down style") unless you are instructed to write in all capital letters. Indicate a new paragraph by skipping an extra line or by indenting five spaces. Avoid words or combinations of words that are hard to read aloud, likely to confuse the listener, or likely to be misread by the newscaster. Put pronunciation guides in parentheses after difficult words or write the guide in pencil above the word. Underline any difficult word with a wavy line.

Bad:

Lady Cholmondeley wore a quartz wrist watch.

Better:

Lady Chalmondeley (CHUM-lee) wore a watch on her wrist.

Best:

Ask yourself if there is any need to mention the watch she was
wearing at all.

Write one story to a page. Do not split words between lines or
sentences or paragraphs between pages. Indicate a second page to a
story by typing "First Add" at the end of the slug. Indicate the
end of a story with the "⊀" mark in the centered on the page a couple
of lines below the last line of copy.

Broadcast news is timely; there is no need to continually write
"today" in your copy.

Weak:

The mayor began his re-election campaign today.

Better:
The mayor has begun his re-election campaign.

As in all writing, avoid the passive voice:
Weak:

A re-election campaign has been begun by the mayor.

Better:

The mayor has begun his re-election campaign.

In selecting verbs choose present or present progressive tense
first, use present perfect if present tense does not work, and use
past tense as a last resort:

Weak:

The mayor began his re-election campaign today.

Better:

The mayor has begun his re-election campaign.

Best:

The mayor is launching his re-election campaign.

Note that when you use the past tense, you must specify the time--for example "today."

Here is a summary of radio news writing rules listed in the Broadcast Writing textbook:

1. Write less formally than for print.
2. Read copy aloud to check for difficult to pronounce material.
3. Cut out puns, tongue twisters, alliteration, and "clever" writing.
4. Avoid gruesome details.
5. Put qualifying statements at the start of sentences.
6. Put transitional statements at the start of sentences.
7. Keep stories brief--less than 20 seconds without audio cuts, less than 50 seconds with audio cuts.
8. Avoid lists.
9. Round off numbers.
10. Write "one," not "a" in "one hundred" and similar numbers.
11. Use titles and names of organizations in full. Organizations usually referred to by their initials (for example, the C-I-A) should be first referred to by their full title, then use initials in the later mentions. Use dashes, not periods, between initials (for example, F-B-I). Avoid any but the best-known acronyms. Write acronyms without periods or dashes (for example, NATO.)

12. Use no symbols. For example, write "5 dollars and 20 cents," not "$5.20," Use no abbreviations except Mr., Mrs., Ms., and Dr., and Ft., and St., in place names.

Keep in mind that rules can vary from station to station. For example, all-news stations have different needs than stations that broadcast news only once every hour.

Figure 8.1 shows you the correct format to use for writing radio news. Study it carefully.

(1.)   (31 lines)

TITLE -- PROGRAM -- DATE -- WRITER'S NAME

Set margins at 10 and 80. (Others may be specified.) Double
or triple space. Use down style (unless instructed to use all
capital letters). Skip an extra line instead of indenting for
paragraphs.

The slug (story title, etc.) goes about one-and-one-half inches
from the top of the page. (Instead of the single-line slug
used above, many stations use a 4-line, single-spaced block
slug, typed at the left margin, one-and-one-half inches from
the top.) Start your story about one inch below the slug.

Never split a word between 2 lines. If a word is too long to
complete on the line on which it was begun, never use hyphen-
ation, as was done here to divide the word. Cross out the ~~por~~
portion of the word you have written (as was done above), and
begin it over at the start of the next line.

Write only one story to a page. If it can . . . not . . . be
completed on one page, do . . . not . . . split a paragraph or
a sentence between 2 pages. With at least one inch left at
the bottom of the page, type "MORE" at the center of the bottom
of the page, and circle it was was done here.

MORE

116

2.

TITLE -- PROGRAM -- DATE -- WRITER'S NAME -- FIRST ADD

The second-page slug is identical to the one on the first page except that it ends in "FIRST ADD." Should there be a third page, it would be the "SECOND ADD," and so on.

Type in a <u>pronunciation</u> (pro-nun-see-AY-shun) guide for any difficult words or <u>pencil</u> one in later. Pencil a <u>wavy</u> line under any tough words.

Underline any words that need special <u>emphasis</u>. Pencil a circle around anything on the script not meant to be read aloud.

Pencil the total number of lines (or running time if so instructed) for your story in the upper right-hand corner of the first page. Pencil page numbers in the upper left-hand corner after the script has been assembled in its final version.

Set off the word . . . not . . . with dots so the newscaster can . . . not . . . miss it. Use the symbol "#" to indicate the end of the story.

NEWS FOR PUBLIC RADIO

Public radio stations tend to use somewhat longer stories than do commercial radio stations. Programs such as "All Things Considered" can give a student a good idea of the kind of story to prepare for public radio. Keep in mind, however, that you should be able to write for whatever station you go to work for. Don't forget how to write the very brief stories used on commercial radio just because you may now be writing for a public radio station. Study all radio news programs--on commercial and public stations--for both their virtues and their weaknesses.

A great advantage to public radio for students is that it gives you a better chance of getting your stories broadcast nationally than would most commercial stations. NPR is a good market for well-written and well-produced stories by writers who have not yet established a national reputation.

COMMENTARY

Commentary is not editorializing. Editorials represent the official views of station management. At this writing, public broadcasting stations are not allowed to editorialize. Commentary is the personal statement of one person on a topic. While it can be a kind of editorial, it functions best as an analysis of an issue. It informs rather than persuades.

Careful research is essential to any good commentary. Examine as many good sources on the topic as you can. It is bad writing--not to mention plagiarism--simply to repeat something you have gotten from a magazine or similar source. Examine each major viewpoint on an issue, and whether you agree with it or not, try to knock it down. See what stands up under criticism. Be particularly hard on the view to which you are most partial.

As in all broadcast writing, keep your copy simple and uncluttered and keep your copy within assigned time limits.

Whether you are writing broadcast news or commentary, keep in mind that everything you say must be understood by the listener. There is no second chance to check what was said. Write clearly and make every word count.

In the space provided below, write the following wire story in correct news format. Copy it word for word; do not worry about style. Be sure to change from all capitals to down style.

VETERAN BOSTON RED SOX FIRST BASEMAN HAL FRENCH HAS SUFFERED A HAIRLINE FRACTURE OF HIS RIGHT MIDDLE FINGER.

THE RED SOX ALSO AWAITED WORD ON THE RESULTS OF X-RAYS TAKEN ON THE INJURED LEFT ELBOW OF FIRST BASEMAN CAL STURGIS.

FRENCH. . .WHO HAD JUST RETURNED TO THE LINEUP AFTER BEING SIDELINED TWO WEEKS WITH A SHOULDER PROBLEM. . .SUFFERED THE INJURY LAST NIGHT AT KANSAS CITY WHEN HE TRIED TO CATCH A POP FLY. TOMORROW'S EXAMINATION WILL DETERMINE HOW LONG FRENCH WILL BE SIDELINED.

EXERCISE 8.2

Each line of a radio news script should take approximately four seconds to read. Correct any errors in the story below, and edit out roughly two lines of copy so that the script is shortened by approximately eight seconds of reading time. Write directly in the workbook.

COLLIER -- 10 O'CLOCK SUMMARY -- 6/4/85 -- JONES 12 lines

Banker David Collier's trial on charges of grand theft and forgery was transferred today to the Milbank Superior Court. No change was made in Collers trial date, which is still set for June 27th. The Conty prosicuter and Collier's attorney both agreed on the move to Milbank. The trial had oginally been scheduled for Evansville. Collier is accused of forging checks onl accounts of wealthy patfons of the Evansville Commercial Bank he is president of that bank until he resigned last monht. Collier denies forging those checks but has pad the bank the full amount of the missing money. None of the alleged victims of the forferies pressed charges against Dollier, but the District Attorney's office decided to file charges any way.

EXERCISE 8.3

Choose a newspaper story at least four column inches long. In the
space provided below, rewrite it as a 40-second (10 line) radio
news story.

When you have completed the story, reread Chapter Eight,
checking your story against the rules set out in the chapter. Be
sure that you read the story aloud to yourself. Check your reading
time to see if it coincides with your estimate based on line count.
Now prepare a second draft of the story, and turn both drafts in
to your instructor.

EXERCISE 8.4

Daniel Stephens was awarded the 1977 Pulitzer Prize and the Bancroft Prize for his book on slavery and race relations. The extract that follows is part of an address given by Stephens. Assume that the speech was delivered on your campus last night. In the space provided after the extract, write a 40-second (10-line) radio news story about the speech. Paraphrase everything in the speech that you use. Do not use direct quotes. The audience cannot see quotation marks, and attempts to use direct quotes usually succeed only in confusing the audience. If you must quote some phrase directly in order to do justice to the speech, precede the phrase with some statement such as, "in Stephens' words."

The separation between the sexes emerges as a result of the industrial process, as most men work away from the home. Therefore you have a spatial separation, as well as a psychological separation between the work of women and the work of men. This gives the women the authority and the locus of the home as their special sphere; it is a consequence of the industrial process itself.

But in the process of being in this situation, women also manage to assert their authority: by limiting the size of their family, they enhance their position as child-rearers; at the same time, the rise of industrialization and the rise of the city remove many of the tasks that once burdened women.

In the farm home, women not only had to take care of the children and the house, but also prepared and preserved food, made drugs, soap, cloth, and clothes. These things gradually all leave the home as industrialization proceeds, and women are left primarily with home maintenance and child rearing. They become the "rulers" of the home. They also are supposed to provide a place to which the husband returns for rest, relaxation, and nurturing after his activity outside in the competitive world.

One of the rather significant social decisions that takes place in the late 18th and has its fruition in the early years of the 19th century, is that all this is not something to be done with the left hand, so to speak; women have to be more than just ordinary beings. They themselves must have some preparation and capability for this task. And what one sees by the beginning of the 19th century is an expansion in women's education.

One can document this quite nicely: at the time of the Revolution, literacy among men in the United States was about 85%, if we consider just signing names on documents. Literacy for women was about 40%. This disparity was about the same in the 17th century.

But by 1860, if we go back to the study of 21,000 rural farm homes, the literacy of both wives and husbands was above 92%. In that 50- or 60-year period, women had moved a long way from being looked upon as not needing to know how to read or needing to be educated.

What happens is that all kinds of academies and schools get established for women. When the public school system begins, it is open to girls as it is to boys. The same thing occurs when high schools are established. So there is no disparity. In fact, the earliest figures we have for high school graduations show more women graduating than men, and on throughout the 19th century.

123

There are ways of explaining that, but it certainly doesn't suggest that women were being put down.

College education is exactly the opposite, of course. Women do not go to college. Why? Because they don't need college in order to rear a family. But they do have to know how to read and write and be educated in the basic subjects so they can rear their children properly.

So there is again a connection between the attitudes toward children and size of the family, and women's opportunities as they move into the middle years of the 19th century.

EXERCISE 8.5

Listen to a radio news program. Time each story. On separate pages that you will hand in to your instructor, write a two-page, typed analysis of the number of stories used and the amount of time devoted to them.

EXERCISE 8.6

Tape-record a local newscast. Then get a copy of a local newspaper that contains one of the stories used in the radio newscast. Under-line in the newspaper story everything that was mentioned in the radio newscast.

On separate paper, write a two-page, typed comparison of the two forms of the story, noting what was covered and giving what you believe are the reasons for the differences in the coverage.

EXERCISE 8.7

On separate pages that you will hand in to your instructor, rewrite these newspaper leads as radio leads:

WASHINGTON. . .Higher mortgage costs boosted the nation's annual inflation rate to 8.4% in May, the Labor Department announced Tuesday, but for the third month in a row, the rate remained below double digits and the increase over the last 12 months has totaled only 9.8%.

WASHINGTON. . .In a sharp reduction of the federal government's role in solar energy, the Reagan Administration has ordered the dismissal of 370 of the 959 employees at the Solar Energy Research Institute in Golden, Colo., and has fired its director, Denis Hayes.

ATLANTA. . .Wayne B. Williams, guarded by seven marshals and deputies, was ordered bound over Tuesday to a grand jury that will decide in about 30 days whether to indict him on charges that he murdered Nathaniel Cater, 27, the latest of 28 blacks whose slayings are being investigated by Atlanta's special police task force.

EXERCISE 8.8

Attend a local sports event. In the space provided below, write a
40-second radio story describing the event.

EXERCISE 8.9

In the space provided below, rewrite three leads from the front page of your daily newspaper as broadcast leads.

EXERCISE 8.10

Tape-record a commercial radio network newscast and an "All Things Considered" program the same day. On separate paper that you will hand in to your instructor, write a two-page essay comparing what was covered in each newscast and how it was covered on the two different programs.

EXERCISE 8.11

Pick an issue of particular concern to your community. Research it carefully and in the space provided below, write a one-minute commentary on the topic.

Writing

The basic rules for writing radio news also apply to television news. There is nothing you need to "unlearn," but there is a good deal more that you must learn. Begin by studying the television news format shown in Figure 9.1. Note the very short lines. On a standard typewriter, a television news line should take about two seconds to read. At stations where 6-pitch type is used, the typewriter letters are twice as large as the normal ones, and a line reads in only one second. The left margin for the audio copy is usually set at about 30 on such large-type machines.

The left column of the script page is reserved for cues. The writer must learn the various cues used, as the visual aspect of the script is as important as the words--perhaps more so. The most commonly used cues for television news are the following:

MOC: microphone (newscaster) on camera
SI FILM or *SI VTR/VO:* silent film or videotape with the newscaster's voice heard over
SOF or *SOVT:* sound on film or sound on video tape
KEY: Chromakey
SLIDE: show 35-mm slide

(1.)

ROBBERY -- NOON NEWS -- 2/17/83 -- JOHNSON   12 lines

MOC   Start video cues at 10 on the
                                       left margin.
SLIDE (:04)   Set margins for audio copy at 40
(#A-73: City Hall)   and 75. (You may need different
                                       margins for over-sized type.)
SI VTR/VO   In general, the rules set out
                                       earlier for radio news writing
                                       also apply to television news
                                       writing.
MOC   A few stations till use paper with
                                       a line down the center and the
                                       word "VIDEO" at the top of the
                                       left column and "AUDIO" at the
                                       top of the right column.

A number of basic rules must be observed when writing television
news. One is that your writing should not attempt to compete with
the pictures. Make your copy complement the pictures. It is not
necessary to describe what the audience can see clearly. Keep your
writing lean. You can afford a few more words when the newscaster is
on the screen--but keep in mind that no one wants to sit and watch
someone talking all evening.

This advice does not preclude tossing in a few unneeded words
from time to time. In the right place, a few extra words can give

your audience time to assimilate information. This is particularly important in leads. The most important information should be kept out of leads. When important information must come in a lead, it should come near the end of the lead, never at the beginning.

You may also need extra words to give your audience time to see material on the screen. It is a good rule of thumb to allow at least four seconds (two lines) for each item you want your audience to observe.

Learn your "visual rhetoric." There is a logical sequence in which your audience expects to see material on the screen. You cannot indiscriminately mix different locations or different time periods in a videotape or film story. You need to understand the rules for organizing stories visually so that you can prepare copy that will make it easy to match film or videotape to it.

Learn to think out each story visually as you write it. It is usually easier to orgaize words in accord with visual logic than it is to arrange pictures in accord with verbal logic.

With rare exceptions, you should view the film or videotape before you begin to write your story. The usual sequence is to view the visual material, select the audio segments in the visual material to be used, then write the story. That way you can be sure that you do not call for any material that is not usable in the film or videotape. You also will know the exact timings of the audio material to lead into it and follow it. Learn to keep a rough timing of all important segments of your film or videotape. That way you will not write ten seconds of copy for a film segment that lasts six seconds.

For all broadcast news, you must accustom yourself to writing under tight deadlines. And you must immerse yourself in daily news. You must read newspapers, read news magazines, listen to radio news programs, and watch television news programs. Only by keeping involved in news can you write news.

131

DOCUMENTARIES

The documentary uses many news techniques but covers material in
greater depth than is possible in regular news. Script format may
either be television news or television film.

The most commonly used documentary form is the "actuality"
documentary, which uses actual film or videotape of events to tell
its story. The documentary writer must build his or her script on
the available film or videotape material. The script must be
factual. The writer's task is to provide dramatic structure to
actual events without distorting them.

The writer should begin by having the purpose of the documentary
clearly in mind. The writer must also know how much money and what
facilities have been allocated for the program. For student
projects, you should be particularly careful to keep these limitations in mind.

The next step in writing the documentary is to conduct
comprehensive research on your topic. Research includes checking
what has been written and what has been recorded on videotape or
other media about the subject. It also includes checking out
people who have information about the topic.

View and catalog all the relevant film or videotape. Then
determine what additional visual material is needed. Interviews are
an important part of most documentaries. They, too, should be
cataloged. Then select what segments you intend to use. You can
sketch in your narrative around these. Pay attention to the time
in your program, and try to build toward climaxes within each
segment while building to a major dramatic moment near the end. Keep
your writing brief. Let the actualities tell the story. Where
interviews are concerned, give thought to playing the interview
sound track with illustrative visuals instead of simply using a
"talking head." Keep all interview material in the sequence in
which it originally occurred. Shoot interviewer questions while the

interviewee is present.

Documentaries and news are probably the most specialized of the various broadcast writing forms. They take practice to learn well. Properly used, they can be among the most effective and satisfying forms of broadcast writing.

EXERCISE 9.1

In the space provided below, rewrite the story used in Exercise 8.1 (p. 120) as a television news story. For camera directions, opposite the first line of copy in the left-hand column type MOC. This is short for "Microphone on Camera," and it means that the copy will be read on camera by the newscaster.

EXERCISE 9.2

Each line of a television news script should take about two seconds to read. Correct errors in the following story, and cut out about four seconds worth of copy.

CALISTOGA FIRE -- 6 O'CLOCK NEWS -- 6/18/83 -- MATSUDA   *16 lines*

 MOC

Fire rored through a lumber yard

in Calistoga Beach, last night.

At least 9 firement were injured

trying to put out that blaze. The

fire was finally brought under

control about midnight, after doing

an estimated 300-thousand dollars

worth of damage. Ambulance crews

treated y firemen at the scene.

Three others had to be sent to

Little Company of Mary Hosptal in

Cumberland. Firemen say the blaze

Was started by an overheadted power

saw. The fire destroyed about 75

percent of the building which hosed

the Calistoga Lumbr Mill.

EXERCISE 9.3

Pick a newspaper story that would make a good story for videotape or
film. That is, it must be a <u>visual</u> story. On separate paper that
you will turn in to your instructor, write a 40-second (20 line)
television news story based on the newspaper story. Make a separate
list of the shots you visualize going with each segment of the story.
(In general, shots should not run shorter than 3 seconds, nor longer
than 8 seconds, with 4 seconds a reasonable running time for most
shots. You will probably have about 10 shots on your list.) Be
prepared to discuss your selection of visuals in class.

EXERCISE 9.4

Tape-record a local television news program. Pick one story that is
also covered in your local newspaper. Time yourself reading the
newspaper story aloud and time the running time of the story as it
was used on the air. In the space provided below, list any facts in
the television story that were not in the newspaper story. Then list
any facts in the newspaper story that were not mentioned on television.

EXERCISE 9.5

Tape-record a local news program, and select a brief story from it. Research the story and on separate pages that you will turn in to your instructor, convert it into a two-minute in-depth report for television. Consider and list the visuals you would want for the story.

EXERCISE 9.6

Pick an article from your daily newspaper. Cut it out. With a dark pencil, edit the story until what is left takes about 30 seconds to read aloud. Copy that material into the space provided below, using television news format. Now edit that material so that it conforms to broadcast style and takes about 20 seconds to read. Turn in the original newspaper story with your edited story below.

EXERCISE 9.7

You want to do a documentary on the problems of the elderly in your community. Go to the library and dig out all the information you can on the problem. Prepare a two-page essay on the major problems of the elderly in your community, indicating how you would discuss these problems in a documentary. Append to your essay a bibliography of the research sources used.

EXERCISE 9.8

From the documentary essay you wrote in Exercise 9.7, in the space provided below, list the estimated running time of each segment of your documentary and what material you would use in each segment. Plan your documentary for a one-hour (59 minute) time slot.

EXERCISE 9.9

Based on the list prepared in Exercise 9.8, on separate pages write the first two segments of your documentary on the elderly and turn the script in to your instructor.

Music, Talk, and Interview Shows

Every program needs some sort of script to get on the air, but many
need only a partial script because most of the program consists of
musical numbers or is mostly ad-libbed.

DISC JOCKEY SHOWS

Disc jockey programs are an obvious example of one semiscripted
show. Many use no more scripted material than a standard opening,
a standard closing, and lead-ins to commercials. Here are a few
factors to consider in preparing a disc jockey program:

1. Musical selections. Top-40 programs usually make their
selections from lists published in Record World, Billboard, and Cash
Box. You need to be familiar with all these publications. Lists for
the same week may be different, depending upon which of these publications you rely upon.

2. Clearance. Your station must have a licensing agreement
with ASCAP, BMI or both in order to use most music on the air. Not
all selections are covered by ASCAP or BMI, and not every use of a
selection may be covered by your licensing agreement. The licensing

agency for each cut on a record is listed on the label. Not all selections on a disc are necessarily licensed by the same agency. You must make your music selections with these restrictions in mind.

3. Timing. Playing time for each cut on a disc is listed on the label. The length of each commercial and the time at which it must run is listed in your station's program log. Plan your program by first checking the total running time of your show, then deducting the time of all commercials. Indicate in your script or outline the time each commercial is to begin. Then fit in the selections you want to play in the time blocks between the commercials. Mark "NLT" (not later than) by each selection to indicate the latest time that cut can be played without upsetting the timing of the show. Subtracting the playing time of the music from each time block will tell you how much copy you must prepare or how much time you must fill with ad-libbing.

4. Emergencies. Give yourself plenty of extra material which can be used in case problems cause the loss of a commercial or a musical selection.

5. Format. Use standard radio script format for all scripted portions of your show. Indicate carts using the format for cart material used for news writing.

OTHER MUSIC PROGRAMS

Most other music programs are fully scripted except for the musical segments. If you are writing for a classical music station, be sure to use the news writing technique of marking each tricky work and printing a pronunciation guide with it. You should be well versed in classical music before you try to write for such programs, because the audiences are usually highly sophisticated. Considerable research is often required.

Television music programs vary in elaborateness. The writer's job is to provide the "continuity" material that links the musical

sections together. Often much revision and rewriting is required
because of problems of timing and staging that develop in rehearsal.
The writer must estimate the blocks of time for which to write copy
by subtracting commercial breaks, openings, closings, and the playing
time of the musical segments from the total running time of the show.
This may be difficult if the musical numbers are not prerecorded
because running times may vary from rehearsal to rehearsal. Time
must also be allowed for applause and laughter. Both live television
and television film script formats are used, depending on the program.

TALK SHOWS, INTERVIEW PROGRAMS, AND CALL-IN SHOWS
Scripted portions of these shows normally consist of the opening,
closing, and commercial lead-ins. Usually, the introductions of
guests and the setting out of topics for discussion are also fully
scripted. A closing summary may be scripted in some cases.

The writer must do careful research for writing of this type.
Most writers keep extensive files on people and topics that may be
used on the show. The writer may play a role in suggesting topics
and guests for the show.

Often the writer may be called on to prepare a list of questions
for the host to use. The questions must be interesting, and should
provide an opening for the guest to talk at some length.

The writer needs to understand the purpose of the program. In
most cases, program hosts try to maintain a neutral role, and
questions and introductory material should reflect this. Some hosts
may wish to play the devil's advocate. A few like to attack all
guests, regardless of topic. Some programs have definite political
or religious slants. The writer must see that the copy fits the
style of the show.

LEGAL QUESTIONS

Writers for semiscripted programs need a firm grasp of the laws affecting broadcasters. The writer should not put in the script material that could lead to ad-libbed material that violates the law. One obvious example is sex. Some years ago, hosts on some telephone call-in programs began asking callers to talk about their sex lives. The results were predictable. Very soon, the FCC levied a $2000 fine against a station for broadcasting obscene material-- and program hosts quickly stopped asking about sex.

EXERCISE 10.1

Read two of the following magazines: Billboard, Cash Box, Record
World. Prepare a list of record selections you would use if you
were a disc jockey.

Take the list and check the licensing agency for each selection.
Which records would you be able to use if your station had a
licensing agreement only with ASCAP? Are any selections not
licensed by either ASCAP or BMI? How well do you think your show
could get along if your station was licensed by only one of the two
major licensing agencies?

EXERCISE 10.2

Assume you have a disc jockey show that goes on at 9:00:30 every night and goes off at 10:29:30. Using the musical selections you chose in Exercise 10.1, prepare a script for yourself in the space below for the segment of the program between 9:05 and 9:20. You have one-minute commercials sheduled at 9:05 and 9:20.

EXERCISE 10.3

After each name in the following list, write the correct phonetic pronunciation for the name:

Leonard Bernstein

Claude Debussy

Norman Delo Joio

Gabriel Faure

Alan Hovhaness

Pietro Mascagni

Francis Poulenc

Ambroise Thomas

Dietrich Buxtehude

Leo Delibes

Manuel de Falla

Charles Gounod

Zoltan Kodaly

Amilcare Ponchielli

Gioacchino Rossini

Richard Wagner

EXERCISE 10.4

In the space provided below, outline a half-hour musical television program. Decide who will be host and who will be the guest musical personality.

EXERCISE 10.5

In the space provided below, list ten people you would want to have
on a show if you were the host of a local interview program on
television. Choose people who would be available in your community.
Script a brief introduction for one person on the list.

EXERCISE 10.6

Team up with one of your classmates. Each of you should try to find out as much about the other as possible. Then do a ten-minute interview with you. Be serious about your interviews; try to find things you can interview each other about that would be of interest to a broadcast audience. Script openings, closings, and introductions for each interview "program." Conduct the interviews on audiotape or videotape if your class has such facilities available.

EXERCISE 10.7

In the space provided below, list 10 interesting topics for a talk
show. Then list at least two people you would want as guests to
discuss each topic.

EXERCISE 10.8

Read the most recent issues of Cash Box, Billboard, or Record World.
Assume that you are a disc jockey. In the space provided below,
list 10 selections you will use on your show and then script
introductions for three of them.

Programming

Many programs serve special groups in your community. The most
obvious example of special-interest shows is children's programming.
There are also programs for ethnic or religious minorities and for
the handicapped. The kind of program you select and the format you
use for it will almost certainly be ones we have already discussed.
What you need to decide for programs of this sort is what is the best
kind of program to use. To do that, you must clearly define your
goals; and to do that, you must thoroughly understand the group you
are trying to serve.

CHILDREN'S PROGRAMS

Most writers set out to prepare children's programs that are in some
sense educational. Nevertheless, it is wise to note that most
children's programs on the air are there for the same reason that
adult programs are there. They provide entertainment that attracts an
audience to which the sponsor can sell goods and services.

Whatever your purpose in writing for children, you begin, as you
would for any other form of writing, by defining your goals and your
audience. With children, age is a critical factor. Great changes
take place in what interests the child--even in periods shorter than
one year. You must decide what specific age group you are trying to

reach.

With these elements defined, you can decide which of the many broadcast techniques available will best serve your goal with the audience you have selected.

Based on their age group, you can decide what level of vocabulary and information the children can deal with. The material must be written with a good comprehension of what a child can understand.

Pay close attention to the average attention span of the age group. Most material written for children must be kept brief.

Make use of repetition. It is useful in helping the child learn, and most children enjoy it.

Keep your language simple, basic English, but don't talk baby talk. Don't confuse the child with dialects and slang.

Avoid portrayals of violence. Some children obviously enjoy violence just as much as many adults do. However, it can disturb other children. Moreover, research suggests that broadcast violence may encourage some children to behave aggressively or violently. Your problem is not so much avoiding violence as defining violence. While the topic may seem simple at first glance, you must ultimately deal with tough issues such as great classics and Bible stories that deal with violent subjects. You will have to decide what constitutes violence in sports. There is no definition of violence that will fit all possible situations. You must always review your material carefully to make sure that you have not overlooked some basically violent material. And sometimes you may have to make the tougher decision of whether--and how much--violence may be excused by the purpose it serves.

OTHER SPECIAL-INTEREST PROGRAMS
The usual problem in preparing programs for special groups in society is a failure to carefully define the group and your goals. For example, what is a "women's program"? There are millions of women in

153

our society. Their needs and interests are as varied as those of society as a whole (after all, they constitute a majority of its members). You must define your target group with great precision. Only then can you decide what needs should be addressed and how they can best be approached.

You must also be realistic. You cannot change society with one broadcast--probably not with a million broadcasts. You need to determine what you can do.

One point to keep in mind for special-interest programming is that the means of measuring success may be different from those used for other programming. A large audience is not always your goal. That does not give you a free hand to do as you please. You must set up alternative methods to see that your defined goal is being reached. Usually the best system is some sort of well-planned polling technique, although this calls for skilled personnel to set it up and carry it out.

And you must never forget the basic techniques of writing for broadcasting. Performing a service does not excuse making a program slow-moving, dull, or hard to follow. Poor writing is never excused on the basis of good intentions.

Radio Programming for the Blind
For example, you can use radio to provide specific services to the blind. Think of the things the sightless person is deprived of. Even if you simply focussed on the daily newspaper, you would realize that being unable to see the newspaper means a loss of many things-- news, puzzles, pictures, stock reports, weather reports, comics, advice columns, opinion columns, editorials, advertising, and so on. The sightless may have other sources for some of this information, but you may be able to provide a needed service. You cannot replace the whole newspaper. You can only fill one of its functions at a time--and that only partially--so be sure your goal is realistic.

Women's Programming

As we pointed out, the term "women's programming" is too broad. You need to determine which groups of women you wish to reach. Then you can analyze the particular needs of those groups. That, in turn, will help you decide which medium and which type of programming to use. Traditional women's programming has included soap operas and shows that have provided advice on cooking or home management. Those categories, along with programs on diet and exercise, remain popular, but talk shows on serious subjects also have large audiences. Give some thought to programming that might appeal to women today.

INSTRUCTIONAL PROGRAMMING

Radio and television can be excellent teaching devices. Again, you must first define your audience and your goals. Beyond that, you should keep in mind the natural limitations of the broadcast media. Most teaching via the electronic media needs to be backed up with printed material to which the students can refer and which they can study. Be sure that you repeat important points several times in your script and summarize key points periodically. If you are writing for television, make full use of the screen to illustrate the subject matter and provide written reinforcement of the spoken material. Remember, too, that you do not have a captive audience in a classroom. The material must remain interesting, or your students will find something else to watch almost as quickly as any other audience would.

ETHNIC PROGRAMMING

Ethnic programs often differ from regular programs more in emphasis than in type. People like news, comedies, dramas, and soap operas whatever their ethnic background. But what the audience expects people to do and talk about on ethnic programs will differ according to the experiences of the audience. Ethnic news, for example, concentrates more on the specific problems and accomplishments of members of the ethnic community than does regular news. The former may also give more prominence to news from the ethnic homeland than do regular news programs. Ethnic programming need not be in a foreign language, but it must be geared to the thinking and needs of the ethnic group to which it is directed.

RADIO AS A SPECIAL-INTEREST MEDIUM

Radio programming can be particularly useful in serving specific audiences because radio has ceased to be a mass audience medium and now directs its programming to specific groups. Radio is less expensive than television and requires a smaller audience to justify its cost. The latest trend seems to be the development of special-interest networks.

THE AUDIENCE AND THE MEDIUM

The radio and television audience has been analyzed probably more thoroughly than any other audience in history. You should find ample data available to help you in planning your use of these media. You can find the age, sex, race, education, and economic status of those who listen to specific stations or use the media at specific hours. All these data should help you target your audience. Study these data carefully before preparing a special-interest program.

To summarize: Define your audience. Define your goals. Select the medium and the technique, then begin your script. Finally, set up methods for determining if your goals are being accomplished.

EXERCISE 11.1

Watch several editions of "Sesame Street." Time the running length of each skit. Note how many times specific words are repeated in each skit. On separate paper, prepare a short "Sesame Street" segment to teach children the colors pink and gray. Use live television format.

EXERCISE 11.2

Watch "Captain Kangaroo" and "Mr. Rogers' Neighborhood." On separate pages that you will turn in to your instructor, write a two-page comparison of the two programs. Note similarities and differences, and state why you think these differences exist.

EXERCISE 11.3

In the space provided below, list ten groups of women in your community who would be logical target audiences for a women's program. Then pick one group and list its specific needs. Indicate the needs you think could best be filled by a radio program.

EXERCISE 11.4

On separate pages that you will turn in to your instructor, write a 10-minute radio program to serve the needs of the group you selected in Exercise 11.4.

EXERCISE 11.5

In the space provided below, list 10 radio and television programs in your community that serve the needs of special groups. Which one does the best job, which the worst job? Why?

EXERCISE 11.6

In the space provided below, outline changes you would make in the program in Exercise 11.5 that you felt did the worst job.

EXERCISE 11.7

On separate pages that you will turn in to your instructor, write a 10-minute "pilot" script for either radio or television, showing how you would serve a group that could benefit from a special-interest program. It should be a group not currently being served by broadcast programs.

EXERCISE 11.8

In 1979 an FCC study group recommended that stations be required to set aside a specific amount of time each week for educational programming for children. Assume you are a member of the FCC. In the space provided below, write a brief report (about 250 words) giving your recommendations and the reasons for those recommendations.

EXERCISE 11.9

Pick a group in your community that could benefit from special programming. In the space provided below, write a proposal describing the program.

THE JOB 12

Writing is a job, an occupation. The writer may be a salaried employee or a freelancer, but the writer is someone who does a professional job and is paid for it. You can write almost anywhere, but most writers work in an office and keep nine-to-five hours just like anyone else. Some writers find they do their best work when they team up with other writers. Some writers work under contract to a specific program, and many programs put regular writers on the staff as producers or in a similar capacity.

If you are writing for network programs, you will probably have to join the Writers Guild after you have sold your first script. A number of other unions also represent writers. Which union you must join depends on where you work and what your job classification is. While it may be difficult to join some unions, most will accept anyone management seriously wants to hire. The Writers Guild itself makes no attempt to exclude new members.

Script assignments normally come from a producer, who suggests the story line. The writer is paid to prepare a ten-page treatment for the producer. If the producer likes the treatment, the writer then does a completed script for which he or she must be paid whether it is used or not. The writer is obligated to do one rewrite if the producer requests it. Other writers may then revise the script.

Some writer is involved from inception almost to the moment a show goes on the air.

It is important for a young writer to be willing to take the low-level, small-town jobs that prepare him or her for the "major leagues." Very few writers start with big shows. You should also have a good collection of scripts and treatments ready to show before you start trying to sell your scripts. No one is interested in "an idea" you may have. They want to see if you can write. If you want to write comedy or drama, it is important to have an agent. However, don't rush into a contract with an agent or anyone else. You may have trouble finding a good agent to handle your work. The agent will want to see what kind of work you produce--preferably material that has been on the air. All material submitted to agents or producers should be accompanied by a standard release form.

There are, of course, many forms of writing besides comedies or dramas. News writing is exciting and is good training for young writers. It forces you to work rapidly and strive for clarity. And it permits you to turn out far more air copy than most other forms of writing. To be a newswriter, however, you must want to read, write, and think news 24 hours a day. It is not a job for people who don't like to read the morning papers. It also can demand odd working hours.

Advertising copywriting is another field in which a young writer can gain experience and make a good living. It helps in advertising if you also have a good knowledge of writing for print. Your job, of course, is to sell the product, which means doing your best even for products that don't interest you. Advertising copywriting is wonderful discipline for a writer because it demands that you get your message across in the briefest time.

There are dozens of other writing jobs in broadcasting. You may do research and copywriting for a talk show. You may prepare material for a disc jockey show. You may provide copy for special-interest programs serving the needs of special groups in your community.

One way to get started in broadcast writing is to work as an intern at a station. You will probably be confined to very unimportant tasks, or simply to observing, but you will be working with professionals and "learning the ropes"--not to mention making useful contacts. Some stations may also accept volunteer workers either full-time or for special projects.

If your school has a radio or television station, you have an opportunity to get experience in broadcasting while you are still a student.

The keys to finding a job in broadcast writing are to set reasonable goals and to be persistent. Be willing to start in low-level jobs. And, whatever you do, keep writing. If your first job does not call for writing (if you start as a page or in a mailroom, for example), write something every night before you go to bed, or get up an hour early and write something before you start to work.

If you have talent, persistence will pay off. There are thousands of jobs for broadcast writers. You may work in a big city or a small town--with a station, a network, or an advertising agency. You may write ads, documentaries, dramas, or news. It's a big field. If you are a good writer, there is a place in it somewhere for you.

EXERCISE 12.1

With the approval of your instructor, choose a broadcast writing job in your community and interview one of the people working in that job. Take careful notes; use a tape recorder if possible. Among other things, find out how your interviewee prepared for the job, what his or her first job in broadcasting was, and how the job was obtained. Find out whether your interviewee has an agent. If so, how was the agent chosen, and how useful does the interviewee think the agent is. To which unions must your interviewee belong? Was it difficult to obtain union membership? You should be able to come up with plenty of questions in addition to these.

After the interview is completed, prepare a five-minute radio script presenting a profile of your interviewee. If you were able to tape-record the interview, include some of the tape in your script. Turn in your script to your instructor.

EXERCISE 12.2

Imagine a job you would like to apply for that relates to broadcast writing. What would a potential employer like to see in your letter of application? In the space provided below, write a letter applying for the job.

EXERCISE 12.3

In the space provided below, list several broadcast-related organizations in your area that take interns or volunteer workers. (If
possible, interview an intern or volunteer.) Now write a brief
portion (2 minutes long) of a radio documentary about interning or
volunteering with that organization.

EXERCISE 12.4

In the space provided below, list five employers in your community
or nearby who might have entry-level jobs for people who want to
make broadcast writing a career. Try to interview the person in
charge of hiring for each employer. Add to your list what openings
there are and what the employers look for in those they hire.

EXERCISE 12.5

On separate pages that you will turn in to your instructor, list five broadcast writing jobs you would particularly like to hold. Then type a three-page essay describing how you would go about obtaining one of those jobs. Make two copies of the essay. Remove your name and anything else that would identify you from one copy. Mark <u>that</u> copy with an identifying code supplied by your instructor.

EXERCISE 12.6

Your instructor will distribute the code-marked copies of the essays prepared in Exercise 12.5 so that no one receives the essay he or she wrote. Read over the essay you received. On separate paper that you will turn in to your instructor, write a critique of the essay, noting what you think was good about the approach and what you think was omitted or should have been done differently.

EXERCISE 12.7

You will have to prepare a job resume to apply for jobs in broadcast writing. Confer with your instructor and check the library for good examples of what a resume should contain.

In the space provided below, list what a potential employer might want to see in your resume. Now try writing a resume. Look it over and see how it can be improved. Practice several resumes before you apply for a job.